COUNTRY FURNITURE OF EARLY AMERICA

COUNTRY FURNITURE

by Henry Lionel Williams

OF EARLY AMERICA

New York: A. S. Barnes • London: Thomas Yoseloff Ltd.

A.S. Barnes and Company, Inc.
Cranbury, New Jersey 08512

Thomas Yoseloff Ltd
108 New Bond Street
London W1Y OQX, England

ISBN: 0-498-06008-X
Printed in the United States of America

FOREWORD

THIS BOOK IS ADDRESSED TO THOSE COLLECTORS AND RESTORERS OF THE SIMPLER KINDS OF furniture made by American craftsmen in Colonial times and shortly thereafter; to the modern worker in wood who delights in reproducing such pieces, and the mere dilettante who finds the study of such examples of pioneer art a gratifying experience affording a rewarding insight into a colorful phase of our history.

Here are notable examples of things of beauty and utility, worth preserving for themselves as well as for what they represent; things that might well have a place in today's homes and constitute a source of ideas for modern furniture pieces and accessories that today's craftsmen can exercise their creative ability upon.

Each example of the early American joiner's and cabinetmaker's art displayed here has been selected for its excellence of design and construction as well as being representative of a type or pattern, or perhaps as a unique variation of a style, worthy of inclusion as an example of ingenious adaptation. In addition to photographs of these pieces, drawings of significant details are included.

No two of these handmade pieces are quite alike, and some of those shown are scarce items to be found only in museums and collections. In such cases, the only way to acquire a duplicate piece would be to make it by hand—a field in which we have indulged ourselves extensively over the years—an undertaking that, executed carefully in old wood, can bring lasting rewards.

In the collection of this material—photographs and information—we are particularly indebted to:

Henry P. Maynard, Curator of American Arts, Wadsworth Atheneum, Hartford, Connecticut; James Biddle, Associate Curator in Charge, American Wing, The Metropolitan Museum of Art, New York; Thompson R. Harlow, Director, The Connecticut Historical Society, Hartford, Connecticut; John S. Williams, President, The Shaker Museum, Old Chatham, N. Y.; Kenneth Wilson, Curator, Old Sturbridge Village, Massachusetts; and Gordon Dyer, Antiquarian, Hadlyme, Connecticut.

Those photographs whose source is not otherwise acknowledged were taken by the author.

CONTENTS

PHOTOGRAPHIC CREDITS

COUNTRY FURNITURE OF
EARLY AMERICA

INTRODUCTION

COUNTRY CRAFTSMEN OF YESTERYEAR

There are two kinds of old-time country furniture—that made by trained craftsmen, and that made by journeyman carpenters and by householders for their own use. It is the first type of furniture with which we are concerned here; the well-made, well-designed pieces put together by skilled workers for everyday use. Herein lies the distinction between the "common" pieces and the "country" pieces, and it is the latter which command a ready market today among discriminating antiquarians.

Much of the attraction of these pieces lies in the careful, painstaking work they represent; the utilization of the natural characteristics of the material, and the careful craftsmanship with which they are put together to last many lifetimes. The more we examine them the better are we able to appreciate how closely is good design allied to structural integrity. No piece was too simple, or too humble in purpose, to be scorned as merely utilitarian, and each craftsman put something of himself into everything he made. This is why we rarely find any two alike and the reason we cherish them today.

To understand how these things came to be we need to know something of the men who made these treasures for us in a day when the craftsman's first job was to make the tools with which he worked.

In the first quarter of the 17th century the first American colonists, North and South, included skillful workers in wood; men versed in the art of building houses and the making of simple articles with which to furnish them. Among succeeding arrivals were others trained through long apprenticeship in the reproduction of furniture, while still others were specialists in the manufacture of chairs.

11

All of these made furniture to order, using as their patterns designs with which they had been familiar in the old country, or copying pieces that had been brought to America from across the sea. In the Virginia Colony the gentry imported from England the stylish furniture for their mansions, having the plainer and utilitarian pieces made on their own estates for their kitchens and the homes of their retainers. Still later, the establishment of scattered settlements and farming communities provided opportunities for the itinerant joiner who could make simple furniture, both fixed and mobile, to the householder's ideas.

During this time the Dutch craftsmen of New Amsterdam and the Hudson Valley also were reproducing—and modifying—the furniture designs with which they had been familiar, and by the end of the 17th century other European settlers in Pennsylvania were following suit. Drifting down into the tidewater regions, they absorbed ideas from other cultural groups such as the Quakers and Moravians, resulting in local variations in design. With the taking over of Spanish Florida and French Louisiana Territory still other patterns were copied and modified, culminating in the adoption and adaptation of Mexican structural and decorative features as the great Western drive got under way. In the North some furniture came to exhibit a French influence, through contacts with French Canada.

In the 18th century, with the growth of substantial towns and seaports and the generally increased prosperity, came the demand for more and better furniture. In the cities this encouraged the establishment of cabinetmakers' shops, most of which were devoted to the copying of imported pieces. By mid-century, however, samples of the work of Chippendale and others in England, and the publication in 1754 of Chippendale's *Gentleman and Cabinet Maker's Director,* made his designs familiar to anyone interested, and this furniture soon

became high fashion. The leading American cabinetmakers modified these designs and, in some instances, considerably improved upon them. Then, perhaps years later, a few superior country craftsmen turned out copies of the simpler pieces in the less costly native woods, a sequence of events to be repeated again and again as new styles, such as those of Sheraton and Hepplewhite, were introduced.

EARLY BEGINNINGS

The very first articles of furniture made here undoubtedly were chests and stools and shelves copied from those brought from the homeland. But it was not long before simpler Colonial styles were developed, as is well illustrated by the variations in chair details in this country, especially in those of the turned type.

The so-called Carver and Brewster chairs, identified with the Pilgrims, actually are ancient types of Gothic origin, heavily built and thronelike and not intended to be moved. The solid wainscot chairs date back to the late 1400s, the box-bottomed being a Tudor variation and the open-legged ones Jacobean. Windsors of sorts were made in England at the end of the 17th century. These were modified in some respects to meet the Colonial conditions and tastes, including the substitution of the more readily available woods—maple for ash, and so on. Such American white oak as was used was generally quarter-sawed, revealing a distinctive flaky pattern, and a feature of many case pieces is the skillful combination of oak and pine, pine being one of the most important woods used in this furniture, especially in the Northern areas.

Even where its presence is not immediately obvious, pine may be found helping to reduce the over-all weight of a piece, or serving in positions where it is not subject to much wear.

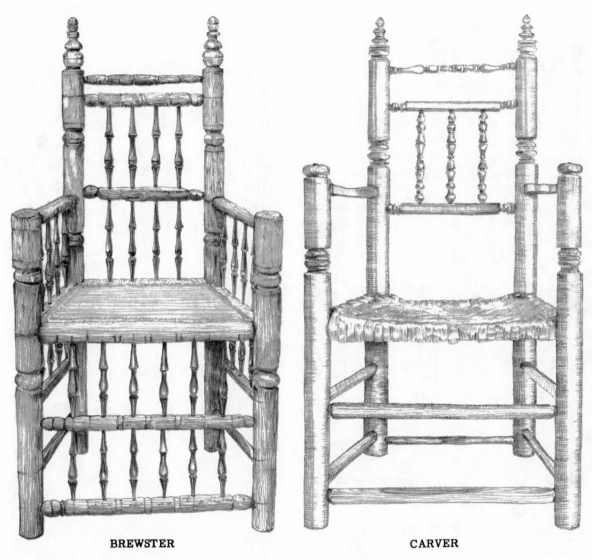

BREWSTER   **CARVER**

Quite often pine tops are used on maple or cherry tables—pine having the advantage of being scrubbable!—while pine backs, pine frames and drawer parts are common. On the other hand, all-pine furniture of the better quality is far less common than often supposed, the trained craftsman having been fully aware that a combination of woods can contribute to longer life and better appearance. Pine turnings, of course, have the disadvantage of having to be made without thin or delicate edges that would break off easily. They are therefore possible only where an effect of sturdy solidity is required.

By the middle of the 18th century, the making of turned chairs for the rural trade had become a specialized business in itself. It called for the use of a variety of woods (often using several species to a chair), and special processes such as steaming or boiling, and bending, the shaping of seats by hand, or weaving in rush or splint. The American

WAINSCOT

WINDSOR

GUILLOCHE

Windsor as we know it today—probably the most generally popular chair ever made—was developed around 1725.

The 17th-century chests made in this country were, more often than not, tastefully paneled, molded, and decorated with geometrically arranged moldings or all-over relief carving in the best English manner. Many pieces were richly carved with everything from Jacobean trail patterns to complicated lunettes, rosettes, hearts, and whorls, or embellished

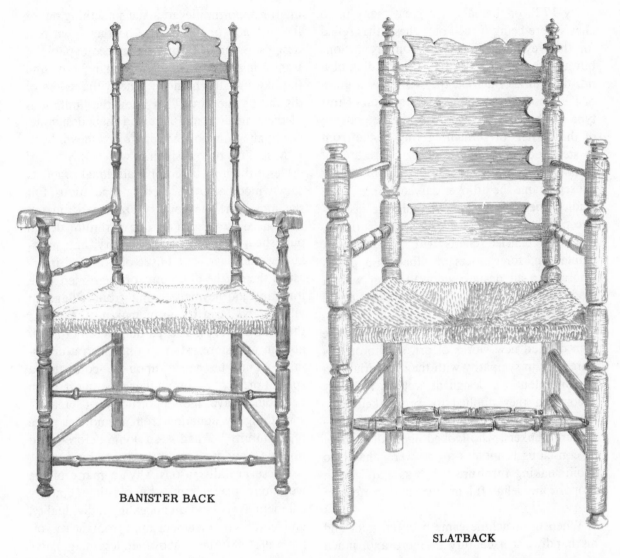

BANISTER BACK

SLATBACK

SPLIT TURNING

with extravagant mitered moldings. But this
did not last. The possession of wood-turning
lathes in the late 17th century that revolution-
ized the chair-making trade was responsible
for a rash of turnery then and later. The split
spindle and boss, found mostly on American
furniture, not only made possible that
much-vaunted American invention, the banister-back chair, but provided the less-skilled
craftsman with a simple means of decorating
boxes, chests, and presses without carving.

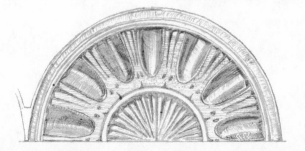

LUNETTE

By 1720 or thereabout a great many plain chests were being turned out; chests that relied for their eye appeal not only on proportions but also the smaller details—the molding of a lid, the quirk of a foot, the well-chosen grain of the wood. From then on, decoration of this type of chest ranged from the simple gouging of the corners or scratch carving of the front to stenciled or painted designs. There are, of course, many brilliant variations. From Massachusetts came the all-over carved fronts of the Hadley chests, from Pennsylvania the decorative panels painted on the flat wood surfaces, and later paneled chests with floral designs painted in, forerunners of other case pieces whose over-all design endowed them with a grace that no applied ornamentation could improve upon.

And so, consciously or unconsciously, these men created new works of art, so thoroughly were they in sympathy with their material—in the unpretentious design as well as the busy decoration they applied to, or worked into, even the simplest pieces. Even the late 18th-century Shakers, who looked upon all thought of conscious beauty as a sin, were unable to avoid making furniture that was exquisite in proportion, delightful in line, and perfection in use.

When the machine came between man and his handiwork a century or more ago, much of this work was lost, or at least abandoned, and is now only slowly being revived for the benefit of the few who can appreciate the work of the true craftsman and value art above price. Luckily for us, there are many examples of the old-time pieces left to feast our eyes upon. And some few of them have been garnered here.

Most of these country joiners or cabinetmakers seem to have possessed a certain amount of creative ability—or at least a retentive memory for the graceful designs of more accomplished workers—plus a hankering for opportunities to make something out of the ordinary or to improve on their own past designs. Some of them were indeed capable of translating designs for mahogany highboys and the like into the humbler pine without loss of dignity or integrity. They knew the limitations of their medium and modified their design accordingly. Some of the results are shown here.

Much of this designing was a matter of "rule-of-thumb," based on traditional practice, slowly modified by succeeding generations. For the most part the country craftsman did not have access to the books on furniture design published during the 18th century, and probably would have found little of practical interest in them if he did. Some of these men were itinerant journeymen, going from village to village and farm to farm; making the things the country people needed that were not available in any store. Many a time such a craftsman would be called upon to construct a special piece of an unfamiliar type; more often he would have the opportunity of creating something by adapting from memory a piece of furniture he had seen long before—and doubtless adding a touch or two of his own.

These are all reasons why so many of the workaday pieces made by old-time country cabinetmakers have an appealing individuality, and features that set them apart from the run-of-the-mill stuff turned out by their less imaginative —and less idealistic—contemporaries. Many of them indeed were, on occasion, afforded the opportunity to create finer pieces in the more fashionable—and expensive—woods such as maple and mahogany, cherry or walnut. How well they succeeded is shown by more than one example presented in these pages.

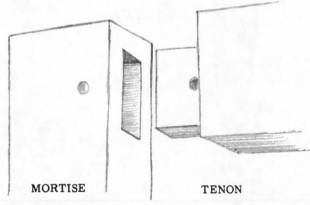

MORTISE   TENON

THE IMPORTANCE OF DETAIL

In the study of antique furniture of any kind it is just as important to know how a piece is formed and put together as it is to understand the identifying features of any particular design. Apart from the fact that the method of construction affects the strength and durability of a piece, it can also serve as a guide to the age and authenticity of that piece. Some of the telltale features of early construction are the size and number of dovetails in a joint, the method employed in joining two boards edge-to-edge; the form of a table leaf joint, the kind of hinge used, the type of decorative molding, and so on. Since these and other variable details will be referred to in connection with a variety of pieces, considerable repetition will be avoided if we discuss them here, beginning with the joints.

FURNITURE JOINTS

One of the most commonly used joints in furniture making (until the invention of the glued dowel) has always been that known as the mortise-and-tenon type. This consists of a tongue (tenon) formed on one stick and fitting into a hole (mortise) in another. With a pin inserted through both sticks this joint can be made almost immovable. But careful fitting of the two parts is essential, and in the old days the country craftsman rarely depended on mere fit. Then it was common practice to make the tenoned part of seasoned wood, and the mortised unit of wood not fully dry. In time, therefore, the mortise would shrink more than the tenon did, making the joint even tighter. It was then held together permanently by driving a hardwood pin through the whole assembly. In almost all cases the tenon is formed with shoulders on two or more sides so that it will remain at a fixed angle with the mortised member.

Variations of this joint are found in table stretcher-leg assemblies and similar constructions. Where the stretcher tongue ends flush with the outer face of the leg, the joint may be tightened by driving a wedge into the end of the tongue. Where the stretcher tenon extends beyond the face of the leg a wedge can be driven through the tongue so that it bears tightly against the leg. In this instance the wedge is easily removable, making it possible to dismantle the table when not in use.

On some quite old pieces a system known as draw-bore pinning may have been used. This was a method devised for tightening mortised joints in a day when powerful bar clamps were unknown. It consisted of drilling a pinhole through the tenon a sixteenth of an inch or so nearer the shoulder than the hole through the mortise. When the tenon was forced as far as it would go into the mortise, hammering home a tapered pin would pull the tenon hole into line with the mortise pinholes, thus

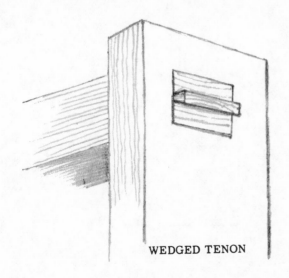

WEDGED TENON

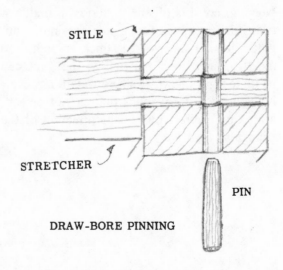

STILE

STRETCHER

PIN

DRAW-BORE PINNING

tightening the shoulders against the mortised member. How common this practice was we may never know, since any such joint taken apart today usually fails to show any signs of such treatment.

The mortised joints were sometimes used in places where they might not at first be expected, such as the underside of cabinet tops. Small tenons were cut out from the top edges of the cabinet sides, and the underside of the top mortised to fit over them. This joint was invisible, since the mortises did not as a rule go all the way through the top—hence the name "blind mortise."

In early tables or case pieces with heavy corner stiles forming legs, both the apron and stretcher are usually flush with the outer surface of the leg. The reasons for this are interesting. Glues were not commonly used before the late 18th century, so that earlier tenon joints had to be made extra large to withstand rough usage. This, naturally, called for larger mortises, and two mortises, at right angles to one another in a leg, might very well weaken that leg unduly. This possibility was minimized by spacing the mortises as far from one another as possible—that is, by cutting them closer to the outer two faces of the leg so that they would not meet. This, obviously, brought the stretcher and apron pretty well in line with these faces. The sketch makes this clear.

Another and familiar type of joint construction much used in these antique pieces is the dovetail—a joint invented by the Egyptians over three thousand years ago. The dovetail, which ordinarily requires neither nailing nor pegging, consists of one or more "fishtail" or triangular members fitting sidewise into triangular slots. If the wood is thick enough, and the two parts are fitted tightly, the joint can be quite rigid sideways. The dovetail, however, is intended to form joints that cannot be separated by a direct pull in the direction of the triangular tails.

In American furniture the dovetail joint was first used in the 1690s for the making of drawers. At that time a single dovetail held each side to the back of the drawer. The forward ends were attached to the drawer front by rabbeting (i.e., shouldering) the front and nailing the sides to it. The shoulder, or lap, then covered the front end of each side member so that the end grain could not be seen, while side-nailing ensured that the nails would not pull out.

A little later someone got the bright idea of combining the shouldered joint with a dovetail, making the drawer front thick enough to allow the dovetail pins' being cut into it. This was soon followed by the use of multiple dovetails —two or three at first—which made a much more rigid joint. At this period the dovetails were widely flared and unevenly spaced, a matter soon corrected in the better furniture. Not until the 19th century, however, were they made flat enough so that more could be used in a given space, with tongues and slots of the same size.

The dovetail joint was, of course, used for many other purposes besides drawers. In the last quarter of the 17th century it was found to be perfect for holding the upper end of a gateleg table to the cross brace that tied the two fixed legs together. This joint could not be loosened by lifting the table by its top. (See **page 61**.) Surprisingly enough, considering the labor involved in making them, dovetails were quite frequently used in making small table and wall boxes, as some of the illustra-

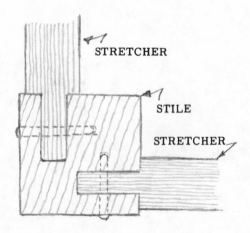

STRETCHER

STILE

STRETCHER

DRAWER

Typical lipped-drawer construction of 1750 or later, showing the multiple, wide dovetails, front and back, and taper-edged bottom housed in grooves in sides and front. Note sawcuts inside, showing front is sawn at angle to miss lip in making joints. Back, sides, and bottom are pine; the front is maple.

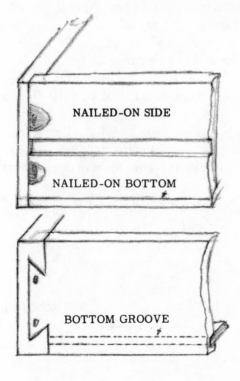

NAILED-ON SIDE

NAILED-ON BOTTOM

BOTTOM GROOVE

tions show. Thin dovetails sunk into the surface were used to tie two boards together in making table and cabinet tops, and repairing the cracked wooden seats of chairs.

Still another important joint in the construction of antique pieces is the lap joint or halved joint. The "lap" is formed by cutting away both pieces where they cross or come together so that the joint is reduced to the thickness of one piece. In the early "sawbuck" type table legs, the lap would be about midway along the legs, and the two fitted tightly together. Either a round hole or a rectangular mortise through both halves enabled them to be held solidly between the stretcher shoulders and a long wedge through the stretcher tenon.

Similar joints which lapped at the ends were often used for the fancy curved stretchers of

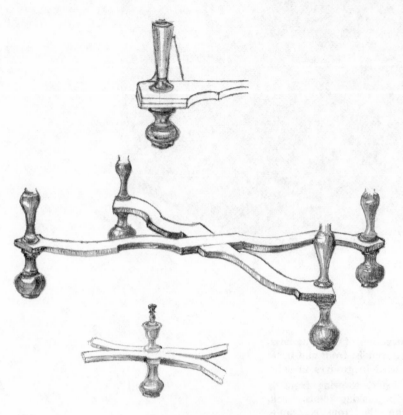

HALF-LAPPED STRETCHERS

receive the squared end of another board. Practically all the old shelves, fixed settle seats, drawer slides, and some chest bottoms were dadoed into the vertical end boards of case pieces. With a modern dado-head or a router, cutting these troughs across a wide board is a simple matter. In the old days, and with home-made tools, it called for both labor and pains-taking skill, especially with a board 18 inches or more across.

The sides and bottoms of boxes are joined together in a variety of ways. In the very old, and cruder, types the front is usually nailed to the ends from the face, and the back attached in the same manner. The bottom then will probably be nailed to all four from below so that all its edges are exposed. Where this happens the better-made boxes may have a strip of molding nailed to the front and ends of the bottom both to hide the joint and balance an overhanging lid. In other instances the bottom may be recessed into the sides, front, and back by forming a simple rabbet on them, with or without the addition of molding. Sometimes the ends of small wall boxes and similar pieces are rabbeted to receive the front and back. This exposes only a thin strip of the sides and enables them to be nailed on from the side instead of the front. Larger boxes frequently have the base extended beyond the front and ends (the back being flush) and finished off with a chamfer or rounded molding.

In the case of applied moldings, the use of a mitered joint seems to have been the rule, but being a mechanically weak joint it could not be used for structural parts unless backed

the Queene Anne style chest-on-frame. These stretchers were normally thin (⅝ to ¾ inch), flat strips of wood, 2 to 4 inches wide but not heavy enough to carry tenoned joints. The laps occur wherever the chest legs center on them. Beneath each lap there is usually a turned foot, with a heavy "dowel" formed on the foot passing up through the lapped portion and into the leg. The curved, X-stretcher used on some such pieces also will lap where the two members cross. In this case the joint will probably be held by a pin which may or may not be part of a turned ornament resting on top, or a foot located beneath it.

Still another structural joint of importance in these country pieces is the plain housed joint. This consists of a groove, called a "dado," cut across the face of one board to

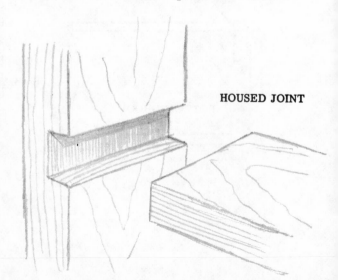

HOUSED JOINT

by a post. This is evident in most paneled pieces where the stiles and rails are tenoned together, with continuous grooves for the reception of the panels and the stiles that separate them. On the other hand, where panel moldings are formed on the stiles and rails, the ends of the actual moldings may be cut at 45 degrees to form mitered angles.

Three common types of joints were used to connect the edges of boards forming the backs of case pieces, including settles, and similar applications. These were: (a) the rabbet, (b) the spline, and (c) the later tongue-and-groove. These were not, of course, structural joints so much as a means of closing a space with a continuous surface while allowing for a certain amount of expansion and contraction.

Still another type of edge joint, more often used on table tops, was the loose tenon, probably a forerunner of the loose spline. In this joint the adjoining square edges of both boards were mortised at frequent intervals to receive a series of "loose" but tightly fitting tenons or tongues. In a much later period dowels were used in place of the tongues, but first came the loose spline. Here, one long strip of wood, called a spline, was fitted into a continuous groove in the adjoining edges. This was followed by the now common tongue and groove which substitutes one fixed tongue and one groove for the earlier arrangement—and makes a much stiffer job. The halved, or shiplap, joint, made by rabbeting the edges of both boards, one from the front, the other from the back, was little used in antique furniture ex-

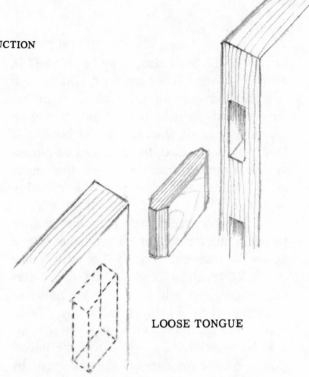

LOOSE TONGUE

cept for the backs of settles or cupboards, as mentioned above.

On very early pieces, table tops, and similar wide surfaces calling for two or more boards, battens may have been used—strips across the backs or undersides, nailed through from the top and clinched underneath. Obviously, this was the roughest form of construction reserved for strictly utilitarian pieces, and in places ordinarily hidden from view. On the other hand, two-board tops will be found nailed to thicker pieces that have been mortised to receive the top ends of trestles. In such instances, however, it will probably be discovered that the edges of the boards are also kept in line by the application of a cleat, a strip of wood that hides

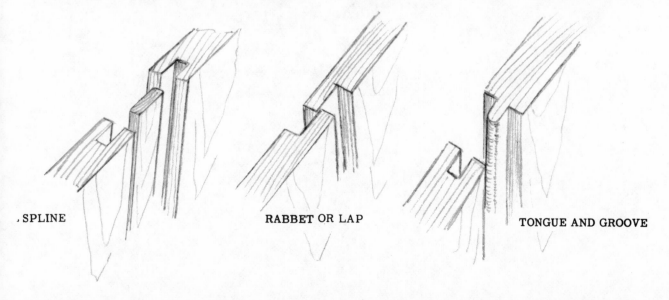

SPLINE   RABBET OR LAP   TONGUE AND GROOVE

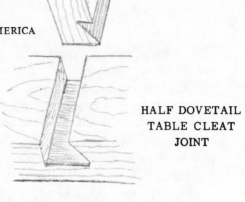

CLEAT

HALF DOVETAIL
TABLE CLEAT
JOINT

the end grain. Such cleats may be attached in a variety of ways. They may be nailed through into the end grain of the boards, or drilled through and pinned, or mortised to receive tenons formed on the ends of the boards. If *blind* tenons are used, the cleat can be pinned or nailed through from the top; if the tenons extend through the cleat they will probably be wedged.

An obvious development from the separate tenons is the forming of a continuous tongue across the ends of the boards. The cleat is then grooved throughout its whole length to fit over this tongue, and held in place by pinning or nailing through. Finally there is the device, used on some tilting table tops, of cutting wedge-shaped grooves right across the underside to receive the edges of the two cleats by which it will be hinged to the base. Each groove will be in the form of a whole or half dovetail, and the edges of the boards trimmed to fit into it. The boards are then slid into the groove from one end and either nailed or pinned through from the top. Board-type stool and bench (form) legs were often attached in this way, braces being added to hold the legs perpendicular.

The subject of fixed joints should not be left without some reference to types of chest construction—a subject that many find confusing. This concerns the difference between "boarded," "joined," and "framed," chests. The boarded chest is the plain box with flush surfaces, made solely of boards even though the end planks may be installed vertically and extended downward to form feet. This may be fastened by nails, pegs, or dovetails. In the joined type the board sides were attached to the corner posts with grooved or mortised joints. The framed chest, on the other hand, consisted of a rigid frame formed of jointed stiles and rails whose sides were enclosed with panels. All three types are illustrated.

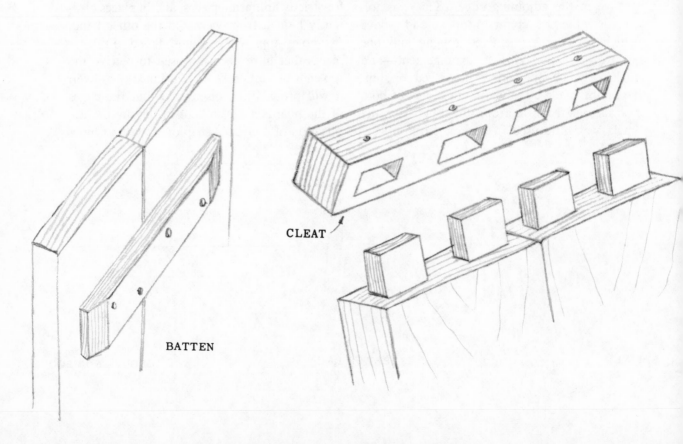

CLEAT

BATTEN

CHEST CONSTRUCTION

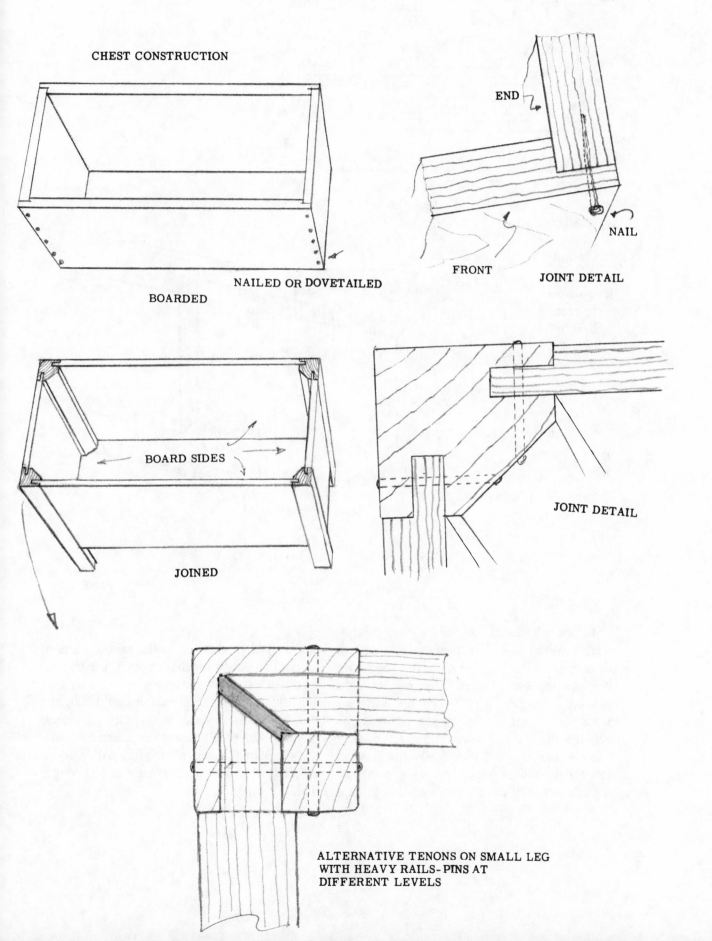

END

NAIL

FRONT

JOINT DETAIL

NAILED OR DOVETAILED

BOARDED

BOARD SIDES

JOINT DETAIL

JOINED

ALTERNATIVE TENONS ON SMALL LEG
WITH HEAVY RAILS-PINS AT
DIFFERENT LEVELS

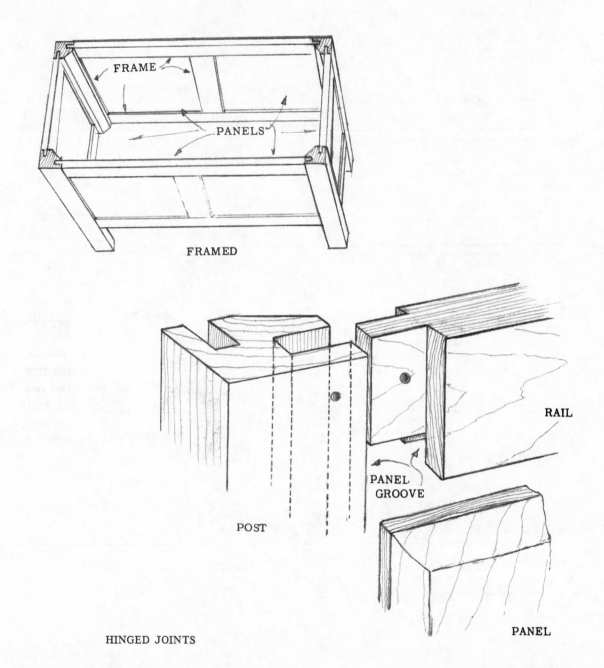

FRAME

PANELS

FRAMED

RAIL

PANEL GROOVE

POST

PANEL

HINGED JOINTS

In the attachment of table leaves, joints were involved that show progressive stages of development. The earliest of table drop leaves had square edges. The butt hinges then used not only became visible when the leaf was lowered, but left an untidy gap between the top and the leaf. The first improvement over this—a late-17th-century development—was the tongue-and-groove joint. This possessed the advantage of having the tongue both support and align the leaf in the raised position, taking the weight off the hinges. Furthermore, with the leaf dropped the gap was mostly hidden by the tongue. Then, around 1700, the rule joint was introduced, exposing a thumb molding when the leaf was down and eliminating the gap. This type of joint called for a different style of hinge having one leaf longer than the other.

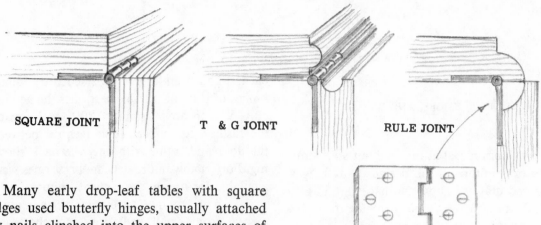

SQUARE JOINT   T & G JOINT   RULE JOINT

Many early drop-leaf tables with square edges used butterfly hinges, usually attached by nails clinched into the upper surfaces of leaf and table. The tongued joints, on the other hand, were held with wrought-iron butt hinges, as were the earlier rule-joint leaves. Later, the hinges were made of cast iron. All of these used the flat-ended, parallel-sided screws. Brass hinges were rarely considered strong enough for use on tables. The principal difference between the old rule joints and the modern ones is that nowadays the curved lip is over half the thickness of the table top; in the old days it was thinner, and often blunter.

BUTTERFLY HINGE

The molding of table top edges also may tell a story, though the humbler country pieces rarely had any such decorative treatment. The commonest type of edge was that forming a thumb molding with a very shallow rabbet and a stubby lower edge. Mostly, the edges had the arrises (sharp edges) rounded off in varying degrees—a process augmented by long wear, while the thicker tops sometimes were made to look thinner by tapering off the underside toward the edge. On some of the later hardwood table tops—Phyfe in particular—the squared edge might be decorated with fine grooves or reeding.

Decorative moldings applied to very early pieces began with the single bead called an arch mold (1640-1710); followed by the double arch (1700-1720), then the channel bead composed of two single beads with a flat surface between them, a scratch bead made from either a flat strip with a groove scratched near edge to form rounded beads, or an arch mold with a scratch bead on either side. Many more moldings were formed on or at the edges of boards with special planes made for the purpose. These produced varied shapes, combining hollows and rounds (as they were called) with right-angle steps formed by a rabbet plane. These old-time moldings are indicated wherever they are of special interest in connection with the pieces described here.

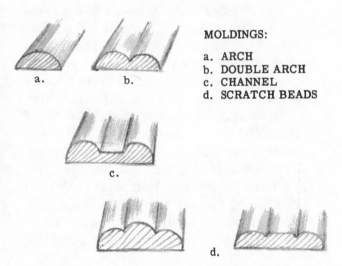

MOLDINGS:

a. ARCH
b. DOUBLE ARCH
c. CHANNEL
d. SCRATCH BEADS

HINGES, KNOBS, AND BRASSES

Few things reveal as much about an antique piece of furniture as the design of its hinges, door and drawer knobs, and hardware in general. And few leave as many telltale traces behind them when they are removed, or look so incongruous when they are· of the wrong vintage.

The earliest type of hinge used on American furniture—apart from the leather hinges of candle boxes, etc.—was the wrought-iron loop contrivance made of half-round wire and known variously as the "snipe," "staple," or "pin" hinge. This was used mostly for chest lids, the pointed ends being inserted into holes drilled at an angle through the chest back board and the lid. The sharp ends were then bent over and clinched into the wood—a rather untidy but effective device dating back to the 13th century.

This hinge continued in use at least a century after the first colonials arrived. It was followed by strap hinges, offset the thickness of the chest back, and "long-leaf" (one leaf long, one short) offsets with, at first, wrapped, and later welded eyes. For cabinet doors the "rat-tail" hinge was an early type, found occasionally as late as 1780. But long before that the famed "butterfly" or "dovetail" hinge had taken over. The early ones were made of thin iron, the two butterfly-wing-shaped or triangular halves looped together. The later ones of heavier metal had fixed pins and welded eyes.

In the early 18th century the availability of H and HL hinges, both imported and homemade, rendered most other types obsolete. These came in cast brass and wrought iron, the former attached by blunt screws, the latter by clinched nails, often with a little square of leather under the head. By this time the butterfly hinges on tables and desks, mentioned

earlier, had been largely superseded by square hinges of thin metal. The cast ones, heavy and clumsy, appeared around 1800, and started the fashion for concealed hinges set between the door and frame with only the back showing. Fortunately, more delicate brass ones were available for use on the better furniture.

A great many American 17th-century pieces, from small wall boxes to chests on frames, have drawers with wooden knobs. Such knobs, of what is known as the clothespin type, were used as late as the early 19th century on certain country cabinets and tavern tables. The earlier ones were made a push-fit in drilled holes where they were held by a wedge in the shank end. Meanwhile, other case pieces would have wider and flatter knobs, with either plain or threaded shanks, a style that culminated in the far less attractive large, thin-headed knobs of Victorian days.

On many of the better cabinets of the 1780s and later, small cast brass or ivory knobs were used, together with hollow brass ones—oval or round—for cabinet doors. On Federal-period furniture the knobs would be hollow ones of stamped brass in decorative patterns. Then, in the early 19th century, pressed-glass knobs in various colors became popular.

The earliest brass handles or, more correctly, pulls, were of the teardrop type familiar on so much early Jacobean furniture and persisting through the Queen Anne period. These and other early pulls were fastened with brass-

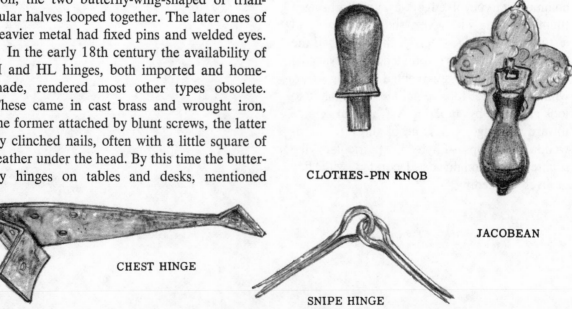

CLOTHES-PIN KNOB

JACOBEAN

CHEST HINGE

SNIPE HINGE

wire "cotters" (i.e. shaped like a split-pin), the ends passing through the drawer front and being bent over into the wood. These drops had little back plates or rosettes, and the keyholes were provided with brass escutcheons which, strangely enough, quite often did not match the rosettes.

Next in line was the Queen Anne type of bail handle, each made up of four parts: a decorative back plate, a looped, bail-type handle, and a pair of screwed (threaded) brass posts drilled to receive the bail ends. Each post after passing through the back plate was held in the drawer front by a somewhat shapeless nut. The sketch makes this arrangement clear. The Queen Anne bails were of fancy shapes, the back plates being decorated with hand-chiseled designs. The lock escutcheons usually match the back plates and are normally the same size.

In the Chippendale-style pulls which came next, the bails were plain and the back plates smooth. Shortly after 1770, with the introduction of Hepplewhite, Sheraton, and Adam furniture designs, the pulls were given oval backplates of thin brass, stamped with classical designs. The bails followed the outline of the plate. These, in turn, were followed at the century's end by circular plates with a ring pull attached at the top edge, by semicircular handles attached at the center of the plate, and lion's-head plates with the pull ring held in the animal's mouth.

QUEEN ANNE

POST & NUT

CHIPPENDALE

HAIRPIN

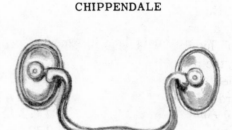

CHIPPENDALE & HEPPLEWHITE

SHERATON-HEPPLEWHITE

EMPIRE

RAT-TAIL HINGE

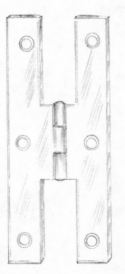

H & H L HINGES

This brings us, then, to the Empire period (1815-1843) after which the country craftsman had little to offer, except in the case of the remarkable Shaker pieces which are a type unto themselves. These are included here because of the continuing appeal of their simplicity of design and beauty of form, a true handcrafted, country style persisting long after the industrial age had made it impossible for the individual craftsman to compete with the machine. On these pieces the wooden knob reached the peak of perfection.

These, then are some of the guiding details to be noted in the pieces dealt with in the following pages. But it should be remembered that in the making of this country furniture there was no urgent need to keep pace with changing fashion; designs were modified slowly so that the Period, as applied to the more sophisticated styles, here means little and dates nothing.

FURNITURE PERIODS

Approximate dates in America

Jacobean	1630-1688
William and Mary	1689-1702
Queen Anne	1717-1745
Windsor	1725-
Chippendale	1755-1785
Adam	1765-1790
Hepplewhite	1779-1800
Shaker	1787-1850
Directoire	1805-1815
Phyfe	1792-1847
American Empire	1815-1840
Hitchcock	1820-1850
Victorian	1837-1880

Approximate dates in England

Gothic	1100-1485
Renaissance	1450-1650
Tudor	1486-1558
Elizabethan	1559-1603
Jacobean (Early Stuart)	1604-1649
Cromwellian	1650-1660
Carolean (Late Stuart)	1661-1688
William and Mary	1689-1702
Queen Anne	1703-1714
Georgian	1715-1793

Approximate dates in France

Louis XIV	1643-1715
Louis XV	1716-1774
Louis XVI	1775-1793
Empire	1794-1830

SECTION I

Benches (Forms), Stools, Chairs, Settles, Couches and Cradles

The first seats were forms (benches) accommodating two or more persons. Seats for one person were the early joined stools which our first Colonials must have used in large numbers. In those days the word "chair" was reserved for a massive structure that we now refer to as an armchair—a piece of furniture reserved for the head of the household. Later on, some of the stools were equipped with a back, forming what we now call a side chair. The stool then became a back stool. For use with the back stools (chairs) by the fireside there might also be small footrests or footstools, and these too could be used as seats.

Keeping the feet off the floor was an important part of comfort on winter days in Colonial homes. This is why most chairs had low stretchers on the front. People using the box settle or a form (bench) needed something else to rest their feet on, hence the footstool. Children sat on them, and so did adults who wanted to huddle up to the fire. A great many of these cozy pieces were made, from the tiny "cricket" 3 or four inches high, to the 8-inch-high Windsor type made of four short sticks and a short plank. The difference between a footstool and a mere stool is therefore simply a matter of size, and the limits have never been defined, though with a full-blown stool it would be impossible to rest the chin on the knees. Joint stools were among the earliest types, and these were usually no more than 18 inches high; often lower. Some of the chair-height joint stools were provided with a small drawer, and the only difference between them and the joint tables was a few inches in height —the tables averaging around 27 inches. From a picture it is often difficult to tell which is which. Examples of each of the aforementioned—the form, joint stool, footstool, the great chair (armchair), and backstool (side chair) are here pictured and described.

The chairs, armed and armless, are shown in what is apparently a progressive but overlapping series of designs. First is the wainscot-type chair which consists largely of oak paneling. Some of these have box seats which suggests Elizabethan or Tudor origin. Those with open seats are more likely Jacobean. A later form of this chair, much more lightly constructed, is **Fig. 7** which has the same wooden seat and heavy turned legs and thick

stretchers. In place of the panel back is a series of four 2-inch-wide vertical strips or "banisters."

Overlapping these and similar joined chairs as to period were the "Pilgrim" types, known respectively as the Brewster and Carver chairs mentioned earlier. These were but two of a series made up of turnings, a fashion developed to a point of absurdity in the mid-1600s on chairs seemingly designed to demonstrate

1

PENNSYLVANIA BENCH

Though the bench (or form) was one of the earliest of seats, this example was made sometime between 1725 and 1750. A not uncommon Pennsylvania type, it is made of yellow pine, painted red, and is quite simple in construction. The top board is mortised to each leg and nailed to the aprons. The aprons, in turn, are nailed to the upper sides of the legs, and rest on shoulders formed on the legs. With this arrangement no other support is required for the legs which are quite rigid. Over-all, the form is 71 inches long, 13 inches wide, and 19¾ inches high. The legs are 1¼ inches thick; the top and aprons a mere ⅞ inch.

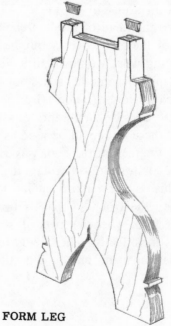

FORM LEG

2

PENNSYLVANIA FOOTSTOOL

STOOL DECORATION

Here is one of the simplest of all footstools—three pieces of plank forming a pair of legs and a top! This painted pine piece is a mere 7 inches high, 13 inches long, and 5½ inches wide. Each leg is attached to the top by a single wide tenon, wedged across the grain of the top so as not to split it. The strength of this piece depends solely on the thickness of the wood. The legs and top are nicely grooved to form emphatic beads, and decorated with paint. This footstool was made around 1800 and must be structurally sound to have lasted so long.

3

WAINSCOT CHAIR

Among the first wainscot-style chairs to be made in this country is this fine example dated sometime between 1630 and 1650. Since "wainscot" originally meant wagon oak it should not be surprising that this chair is of solid oak throughout—oak quarter-sawn in the Colonial manner. A long time ago some less skillful craftsman ventilated the back panel by sawing slots and drilling holes in it, in the manner of an old-time tape loom. The antique leather cushion hides a replacement seat, the only unoriginal part. Note that the top rail of the back has a panel molding formed on it. This same molding is repeated below the seat front and sides. The top rail is tenoned to the rectangular posts which are reduced in thickness toward the top. The turnings of the front legs (which also form the arm posts) are of a very early pattern. The seat itself is finished off with heavy moldings on three sides that terminate at the rear faces of the back posts. The back is 34¾ inches high, 18½ inches wide. The seat is a mere 15½ inches from the floor, and at the rear measures 20¼ inches over the molding; at the front it is 23½ inches. The 1-by-2 stretchers are 3 inches from the floor. The arm posts extend upward 6 inches from the seat to arm, and the arms are 20 inches long. The rear legs are 2½ inches wide by 1¾ inches thick, tapering to ¾ inch at the top. The front legs are 2½ inches on the square—altogether quite a small chair considering the sturdy build.

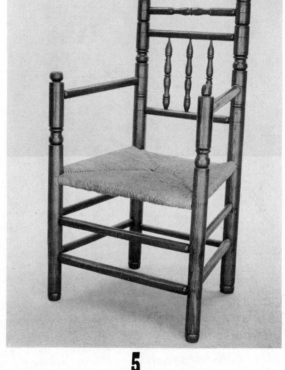

5

CARVER-TYPE ARMCHAIR

4

BREWSTER-TYPE ARMCHAIR

In spite of the fact that turnings below the seat are thought to indicate later construction, this 17th-century Brewster is one of the earlier type purposely made heavy and unwieldy because it was rarely moved. The uprights are of ash 2¼ inches in diameter; the spindles—all 36 of them—as well as the stretchers are of hickory. The plank seat is shown with a loose cushion. Normally, the ends of the spindles and stretchers are not turned, making a better joint in the rough. The stretchers are pinned, but not the spindles. Over all, the chair measures 44¾ inches high, 32½ inches wide, and 15¾ inches deep, the seat being 19¾ inches from the floor as befits a chair of state. Presumably a footstool was necessary, as the lower spindles prevent the bottom stretcher being used as a footrest.

This Carver-type chair, though dated 1650-1700, is of a lighter construction, the posts being a shade slimmer—1 9/16 inches—than those of the Brewster, though the Carver is two inches taller. The principal dimensions are: Height 46¾ inches, width 25 inches, depth 18 inches. It is also narrower in the seat but deeper, with a seat height of almost 18¾ inches. Made entirely of ash, with a rush seat, this chair has almost plain stretchers except for the topmost one. The post turnings are unusually attractive, though the front post balls have suffered damage. Much of the feet still remains, and the lower front stretcher is but lightly worn in 300 years of use. The seat is a replacement.

6

PILGRIM SLAT-BACK CHAIR

Quite as old as the Brewster type chair, though a newer style at the time, this Pilgrim slat-back is of oak with ash splats. All stretchers are plain but the arm rests have an unusually delicate turning. The feet seem to be replacements, along with the rush seat. The three splats are of equal size and shape, and lightly curved. Probably the most attractive feature of this chair is the back-post turnery. Dated late 17th century, this chair measures 45½ inches high, 22¾ inches wide, and 22 inches deep.

just how many spindles and turned rails could be accommodated in one chair. Later in the 17th century some much simpler armchairs were made with turned legs and high backs with wide splats. By the turn of the century these chairs, now seated in rush (and later in splint), had been scaled down considerably in weight, becoming really portable, **even** though the backs had as many as five or six splats.

This reduction in weight and solidity was accompanied by a new trend in decoration consisting of excessively turned uprights, stretchers, and, in some instances, double-bearing arms (arms supported by a spindle extending down below the seat to the upper side rail). Backs now had graduated to bowed slats in various shapes including the scrolled, serpentine, and salamander designs. The less pretentious ones were perfect for farmhouse

and cottage, and so easily made by anyone with a lathe and a pod auger.

In this same period (1700-1720) the true turned banister-back chair became popular. On most of these the four banisters were split, with the flat side to the front. Where these banisters are found with the rounded side to the front it may be assumed that the country chairmaker either had a faulty memory or an irresponsible urge to be different. Other such craftsmen found it simpler to use straight-sided "banisters," perhaps decorated with reeding. All of these chairs had fancy top rails, and perhaps overlarge turnings on the front stretcher. Many also were given the Spanish foot, perhaps with a carved front stretcher, an altogether more sophisticated design reminiscent of the Flemish and Carolean cane-back chairs of 1690 and later.

7

PENNSYLVANIA ARMCHAIR

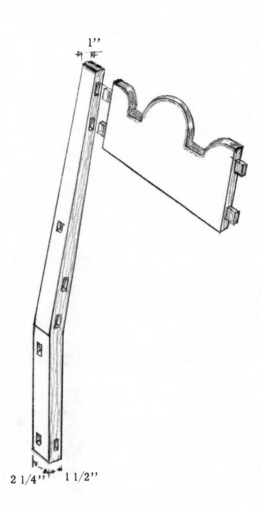

1"

2 1/4"   1 1/2"

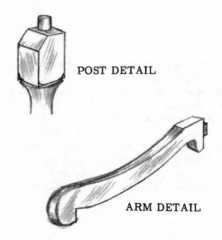

POST DETAIL

ARM DETAIL

Suggesting the earlier wainscot chair, this early 18th-century Pennsylvania-style armchair, dated 1725-1750, makes the best use of walnut, with its ample bearing surfaces for the mortised joints and the arms, plus an interesting grain. The turnings in the same wood show no sharp edges to split off, and the arm supports have a graceful rigidity. Walnut chairs of this type were made from the late 17th century to the middle of the 18th century. One notable feature of this piece is the apparent delicacy of the front legs and feet compared with the heavy back, seat, and rear posts, and the solid side stretchers. It is nevertheless a handsome chair. Note the molded bottom of the apron and bearing of the arms on their supports. Dimensions are: Height 47 inches, width 20⅛ inches, and depth 21½ inches.

8

BANISTER-BACK ARMCHAIR

The American banister-back armchair of which this is an excellent example made of maple, was almost contemporary with the Pennsylvania chair which introduced the plain banister-back type. This one, which has banister-pattern turnings, is dated 1700-1710. The banisters are finely executed split turnings with the flat side forward for added comfort. Here the turner comes into his own again with exaggerated ball stretchers and turned posts. The top rail, with its carved and pierced cresting—well within the capacity of the better country craftsman—tones in nicely with the Spanish feet, while the rolled arms provide plenty of bearing for their delicately turned supports. Four banisters are usual, though there are armchairs with five, and side chairs with three. Note that the cresting is between the posts; in some instances it may surmount them. Dimensions of this chair are: Height 47 inches, seat 25½ inches at the front, 16 inches from the floor. The carved crest is 14 inches wide and 6¾ inches high; the arm 18 inches long.

9

MAPLE FOUR-BACK ARMCHAIR

Beautiful turnings are a feature of this four-back maple chair with its delicately upswept and graduated splats suggestive of a Pennsylvania style of 1710-1740. Once converted to a rocker, this chair has been carefully restored and now stands 45 inches high. The center sections of the flat-surfaced, vertically curved arms, are reduced in thickness for lightness in appearance, but the ends are thickened and solid enough to stand pinning. The back posts measure 15 inches to the outsides, and the seat is 14 inches deep, and 18¾ inches high. Over-all height is 43 inches. The posts are 1½ inches in diameter, and the splats are bowed 1⅜ inches.

10

WINDSOR CHAIR—ABOUT 1830

Windsor chairs—made from about 1720 on—vary so widely in design and proportions, and there are so many of them, that selecting a typical example would be difficult. The one shown here, however, is far from ordinary and constitutes an interesting conversation piece. This wide, shallow chair is of what is known as the hoop-skirt type, but, apart from its shape and the arrangement of the spindles, it has all the structural features that set the Windsor apart from any other chair.

All Windsors consist of a thick, shaped seat into which both the legs and the back spindles are inserted. In this particular example the elliptical seat is exceptionally wide, shallow and only moderately recessed. It is made from one slab of pine with the grain running lengthwise. After being shaped, the seat is drilled to receive the turned legs which are usually of maple or birch, as are the three turned stretchers —in this case the former. The legs may extend right through the seat, as they do here, or only part way. In either case they are wedged in the holes drilled for them. The back is of turned hickory spindles, with the heavy side spindles of maple. The back spindles terminate in a slender comb with saucy ears to form a modified fan back. This chair is 35⅛ inches high, the width being 25 inches at the top and 20½ at the seat which is a mere 13¼ inches deep.

11

12

SALAMANDER SLAT-BACK ARMCHAIR

SHAKER ROCKER

A salamander-back armchair such as this with delicate turnings and exquisite double-bearing arms
would be a challenge to anyone skilled in turning.
The wood is birch and the style shows a French influence via Canada. Chairs of this type have been
dated as far back as 1720, but this one is apparently
of the later 18th century. Though only 37¾ inches
tall, it is 22¼ inches wide and 18¼ inches deep.
Such chairs are occasionally found in Vermont and
New Hampshire, all with reed seats, and apparently
the work of country craftsmen with some skill and a
sense of beauty. A fascinating piece to copy.

This rare five-back Shaker rocker was made before
1830, the mushrooms having been turned in one
piece with the front posts. The wood is cherry with
a splint seat. The slightly curved arms fit part way
around the posts. The "sled"-type rockers are pinned
into the slotted ends of the posts. Only the top and
bottom slats are pegged into the posts from the rear.
All the slats are of ash. The seat is 20 inches wide
at the front and 15 inches at the rear, and stands 15
inches from the floor. The overall height of the chair
is 48¾ inches; and the seat, from front to back,
measures 22¼ inches. On later rockers the mushrooms were made separately and doweled through
the arms into vase-turned posts. This rocker, like
all Shaker pieces, was intended to be purely functional in design, but in the hands of a true craftsman
it also became a work of art—as much as any
rocker can.

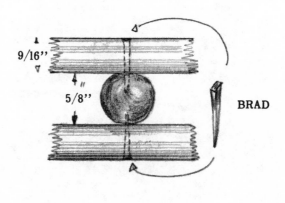

9/16''

5/8''

BRAD

13

DECORATED TURNED CHAIR—1820

The ultimate in decoration in turned and bent chairs is represented by this rush-seated example which seems to have graduated from kitchen to parlor. Painted all over a delicate gray, it is decorated with brown, black, and gold—tiny swags on the back rails and leg rails, leafy sprays on the seat bow, feathers on the uppermost section of the legs, stars in circles on the seat corner blocks, wide gold stripes down the fronts of the legs, and every ball gilded. The underside of the bottom back rail has the name "L. Barnes" burned in. The rails and stretchers are of hickory, the legs of ash.

Actually, much more work has gone into this chair than may be immediately apparent. The back legs are carefully tapered, from 1½ inches at the seat to 1 inch at the top and 1⅛ inches at the foot. In addition, the back is bent 4 inches to the rear at the top. The front legs, which have a short vase turning at the top, are 1½ inches thick just below that point, tapering to ⅞ inch at the bottom. The top ornamented sections are 1⅛ inches diameter where they form a shoulder for the corner blocks. These blocks (1½ inches square and ⅞ inch thick), are nicely rounded off both on top and at the outer corner, and the legs are doweled into them. The decorative balls are held by handmade brads inserted through the rails, both top and bottom. Since the seat is bow-fronted, it measures 15 inches from back to front at the ends and 16¼ inches in the center. The seat is 18¼ inches wide at the front and 15¼ inches across the back legs.

14

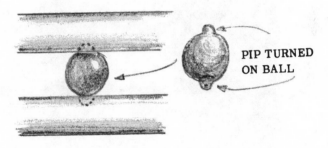

PIP TURNED
ON BALL

FANCY SHERATON CHAIR—1830

Simple maple chairs of a similar type to this, with ball decorations between the turned back rails, were made from about 1820 on. The one shown has the Hitchcock-style back posts flattened above the seat. The front legs are turned, tapered, and splayed outward toward the bottom, and have a button foot. The reeded seat, recent in this example, is trimmed with a wide thin strip of hickory wrapped around it and nailed on. The front legs terminate in shaped blocks, 1 inch thick, drilled to receive them. These blocks hold the shaped front and side seat rails whose ends are rounded to form dowels. The side and back seat rails fit into holes in the back legs. The back rails are turned and bowed, the balls between them being held by small projections turned on them which fit into tiny holes in the rails. The whole of the wood is coated with a semitransparent finish of a dark brown, almost black in color.

Over-all the chair is 34 inches high, the seat 17 inches from the floor. The back is 16 inches wide at the top and 14½ at the seat. Maximum width of the round-sided seat is 18 inches, the depth, back to front, 15 inches, and the legs are 1⅜ inches in diameter.

15

TURNED KITCHEN CHAIR—1841

Of this chair a great deal is known. It was made in 1841 by a Westchester County, New York, coffin-maker, and is in its original condition, even to the rush seat. Plain, foursquare, and serviceable, it has not one shaky joint. The legs are of maple, the slats of oak ¼ inch thick at the middle, ⅛ inch at the ends, and only the topmost one is held with pins which are inserted from the back. All the other joints rely on the original tight fit.

All four legs are 1⅛ inches in diameter, the back ones tapered slightly at the bottom, the upper ends finished with a bead. The front legs have a simple but nicely shaped foot, an uncommon feature on these strictly utilitarian chairs. The chair stands 33 inches high, the seat being 17 inches from the floor, and measuring 14¾ inches wide at the rear; 17¾ inches at the front. The slats are graduated, the top one being 2¼ inches wide, the middle one 2⅛, and the bottom one 2 inches. The rungs are all ⅞ inch in diameter and are not turned where they enter the legs. The original finish seems to have been raw linseed oil, with a coat of very thin shellac added sometime later.

From 1730 on, Spanish and Dutch features were often combined, with questionable results, till the purer Dutch and Queen Anne patterns displaced them. These later styles were readily modified to suit the skill (or lack of skill) of the country craftsman.

A similar metamorphosis took place as, at mid-century, the Chippendale influence began to make itself felt, with walnut and maple and sometimes cherry substituted for the more fashionable (and expensive) mahogany. This was the period during which the Windsor chair gained tremendous popularity—at first used largely out of doors, and therefore painted. These were produced in a variety of patterns too numerous to catalog here, culminating in the Sheraton Windsors with bamboo turnings —a type of chair eminently suited to production by the small chairmaker for country dwellings, and a style just as popular today as then.

In addition to the chairs and stools, many homes were equipped with more or less fixed seats alongside the fireplace. These fireside seats, or settles, were intended to provide a warm corner free from drafts on neck and ankles. The backs were high, and usually extended down to the floor for that purpose. Many were of extremely simple construction; some were curved; some provided with a shelf for a lamp and perhaps for a tankard of ale. Occasionally the seat formed the cover of a storage chest, or had two or three drawers beneath it. Larger settles were often given imposing paneled backs, perhaps with turned legs, and some could be converted into a bed by merely tilting the seat. Quite often these beds consisted merely of a collapsible box into which bedding was dumped. Today they are interesting antiques that serve to remind us of the rigors of home life centuries ago.

The couch, daybed, or chaise longue as it is variously known dates back to the early settlements, being found both earlier and more

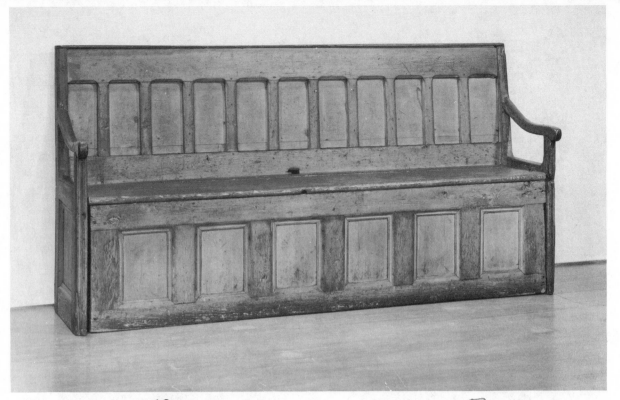

16

PINE SETTLE-BED

Always concerned with the lack of room space, our forefathers devised many pieces of double-purpose furniture of which this is a good example—a pine settle by day, a bed by night. The back panels are formed of one single board. The seat is entirely separate, forming a box with its own ends. When that box is tilted forward so that the paneled front rests on the floor, it forms, with the back section, a complete high-sided box. A feather mattress or an armful of straw in the bottom of this box converts it into a bed—an idea that seems to be of Irish origin.

Although it looks tremendous in the picture, this piece is quite small—74¼ inches long, 37 inches high, with the seat 17½ inches from the floor and 13¾ inches deep. The base is 15½ inches deep over molding and leg. Back posts are 2⅞ inches × 1½ inches; front posts 2¾ inches thick, over the attached ¾-inch molding by 1½ inches wide.

TOP RAIL

CHAMFER

TENON

PANEL

PANEL BOARD

STILE

TENON

BOTTOM RAIL

DETAIL OF SETTLE-BED
BACK PANELLING

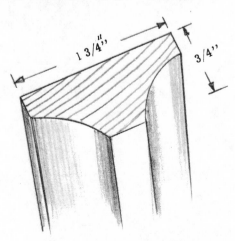

1 3/4"

3/4"

FRONT POSTS

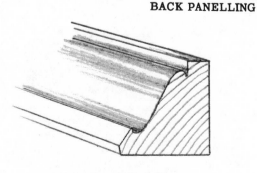

LOOSE PANEL MOLDING

17

OPEN-FRAMED PINE AND MAPLE SETTLE

Here is a framed pine and maple settle with some unusual features including the fifth leg and a back sill of oak. The wainscot-type arms are tenoned to the back and the turned posts. The panel molding being formed on the back posts results in the top rail being let into the posts the depth of that molding. It should be noticed also that all pairs of pins are deliberately out of line to discourage splitting along the grain. The front and end seat rails are finished off with a stone molding along their lower edges. This settle is believed to be a unique Connecticut piece of the late 18th century. Dimensions are: Length 75 inches, height 50½ inches, depth 27 inches. The seat is 20½ inches deep and 20¼ inches high. The front posts measure 2½ inches on the squares, and the back posts are 1¼ × 2½ inches. The shaped back posts are raked 1½ inches from seat level.

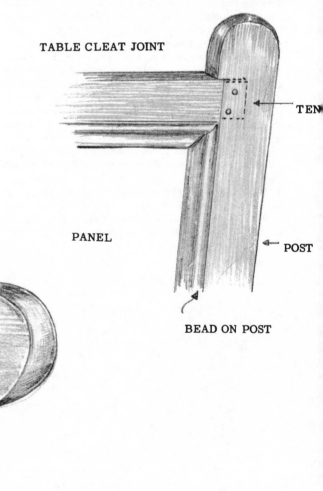

TABLE CLEAT JOINT

PANEL

TEN

POST

BEAD ON POST

PINE SETTLE ARM DETAIL

18

PANEL-BACKED PINE SETTLE

Here we have a craftsman-built pine settle of the late 1700s in almost as perfect condition as the day it was made. The five-paneled back, the bracketed hood, and the sweep of the scrolled arms; the proportions of seat and beaded apron, together with the shaped feet make this a well-designed piece of furniture, as handsome as it is efficient. The back board, extending to the floor, adds to the comfort of the user. This settle, made in the 18th century, is 84½ inches wide, 59 inches high, and 22¼ inches deep.

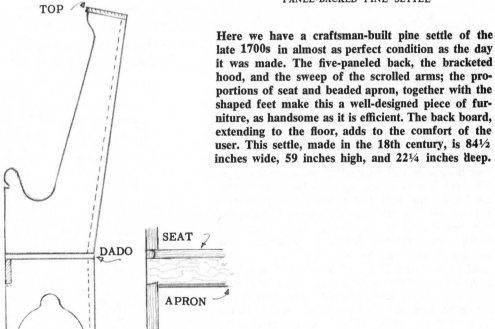

TOP

DADO

SEAT

APRON

PINE SETTLE END

19

PINE SETTLE—1700

One of the simplest types of early pine settles is shown here, in an almost perfect state of preservation. Though plain in design and entirely functional, it fulfills its purpose perfectly which is more than can be said for some more decorative patterns. Not only has it a tall back, with projecting top and sides to ward off drafts, but there is also an enclosed space below the seat for the same purpose. The flat top board extends far enough forward to permit a Betty lamp to be hung from it both for reading and illumination as well as lighting an occasional pipe. The back boards, which are exceedingly wide, have lap joints. The ends are in one piece, with semi-circular arm rests cut out at a convenient height, and they are dadoed to receive the single board seat which is 16 inches deep. The seat is secured by nailing into the ends and through the back.

All of these boards are a full inch thick and show evidences of the round-nosed plane that was used to smooth them. The settle is 4 feet 1 inch long, 5 feet 3½ inches tall; 15½ inches deep; the seat 15 inches from the floor, and the bottom of the armrest 14 inches above the seat.

frequently in the South. Apparently the first couches were of the turned variety, and these continued to be made well on into the 18th century. Many of these had adjustable headrests, but the later and more fancy Dutch, Flemish, Queen Anne, and Chippendale styles had fixed headrests. None of these pieces had a "back" along one side as do some modern couches.

Quite a few of the still existing early couches could be, and obviously were, made by country craftsmen, especially the turned type consisting of four or six legs and a pair of posts. The head could be fixed, like a chair back, or hinged between the posts so that the angle could be regulated by adjusting a pair of chains or straps. The legs and their transverse and longitudinal stretchers were surmounted by a wooden frame which supported the seat. Early seats were of rush or splint or stretched canvas, or even of rope, as in a bed. The heads could be caned, spindled, slatted, or upholstered. Those with a fixed head usually had the posts bent back from two to eight inches, though the late 18th-century types with plain, round posts and stretchers more likely had vertical back posts tied together with flexible

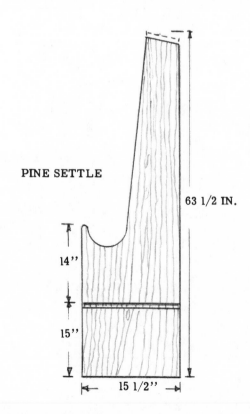

PINE SETTLE

63 1/2 IN.

14"

15"

15 1/2"

20

TURNED COUCH—1725

Six turned legs and a pair of turned posts leaning at an angle; an adjustable back hinged between these posts, form this simplest of daybeds or couches made in 1725 or thereabouts. The piece is of maple painted red, and hails from Pennsylvania. The center four legs are 3 inches in diameter, the end legs and the feet of the posts slightly less. The 36-inch-tall posts are set to lean back about 4 inches. Heavily turned side stretchers and plain cross stretchers space the legs and posts. The seat frame, supported by eight uprights, is shaped to receive a rush or even a stretched-canvas seat. However, it should be noted that wherever such flexible seating material is used, other stretchers are needed between the tops of the inner two pairs of legs. In the example shown, these are missing but the holes to receive them betray their loss.

The adjustable head is hinged to the post by dowels at the lower end, four inches above the seat. This back consists of three vase-shaped splats tenoned into the hinged rail and terminated above by a solid wood cresting level with the post tops. Near the top of each post is an iron staple to which the adjusting chain is linked. Strong hooks in the cresting allow the chain between post and cresting to be lengthened or shortened at will, thus changing the angle. Excess chain hangs down behind the headrest.

Over-all, the chaise measures 67¾ inches in length, 23½ inches in width, and is 36 inches high to the tops of the posts. The couch seat frame is a mere 14 inches from the floor.

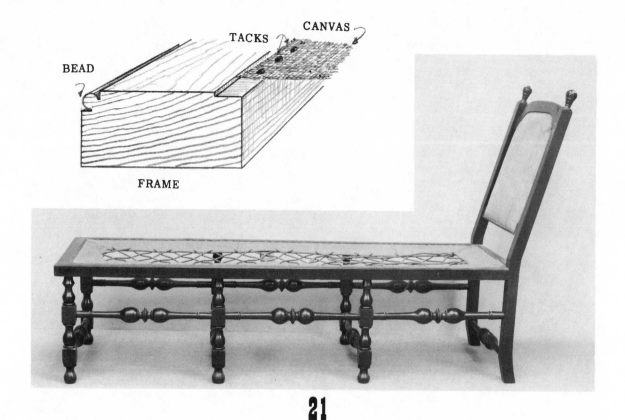

BEAD TACKS CANVAS FRAME

21

TURNED WALNUT COUCH—17TH CENTURY

This 17th-century couch in walnut is an exquisite example of graceful and well-proportioned turnings combined with a frame of equally careful design. The frame members are 2 inches deep and 3½ inches wide, with a shallow rabbet, ½ inch wide along the inner top edge to receive the thick canvas cushion support which is held by a line of heavy tacks. This canvas, about 9 inches wide, it intended to be pulled taut by a webbing of rope, distributing the tension equally in both directions. It should be noted that the back pad is similarly let into the top rail a sufficient depth to accommodate the final upholstery covering material. The lower part of the pad covers the two vertical supports and is finished flush with the bottom edge of the lower rail which is centered in the thickness of the back posts. A thin decorative bead is worked into the outer top corner of the frame, the back posts, and the top rail, adding to the air of refined elegance.

The shaped back posts are in one piece, with the finials turned on them instead of being applied later. The dimensions of the frame and rear-leg post members are heavy enough to make substantial mortised joints possible. The turned legs are blind-doweled into the frame side members. The back posts measure 2 × 2½ inches. The frame is given extra stiffness at the center by a 1 × 4-inch crossbrace set well down so as to clear the tension cords that support the cushion. The over-all height is 3 feet 2½ inches; the frame height 15 inches, the over-all length 5 feet 6 inches, and the width 21¾ inches.

FINIAL

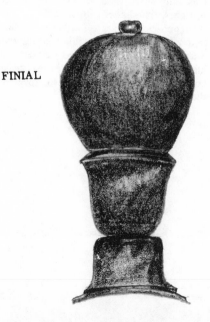

STRETCHER TURNING

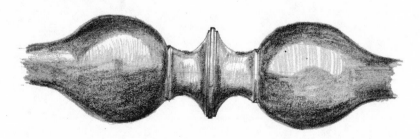

22

QUEEN ANNE DAYBED—1740

This curly-maple daybed is a prime example of the Queen Anne style. Its design features—the shaped cresting, the separate vase back mounted between the back posts as though it was intended to be adjustable (as many were); the hollowed-out lower back rail, and the details of the legs with the centered longitudinal stretcher, all suggest unusually competent design and execution. This has led authorities to suspect it may be the work of Job Townsend of Rhode Island, who flourished at this period. Be that as it may, the execution is still not beyond the capacity of the better country craftsman of the time. One structural feature to note is that the frame side and end (foot) members are tenoned and pinned into blocks formed on top of the legs, making the legs an integral part of the frame.

At the head, the frame members are tenoned into the posts as usual. It should be observed that the whole head assembly, including the leg portions, is carefully designed with sweeping lines and chamfered arrises so as not to contrast too strongly with the curves of the legs and stretchers. Even the back posts are given flowing lines that the square portions only serve to emphasize. The finials, incidentally, are attached by dowels, so that in turning them the whole leg does not have to be swung in the lathe. They are also made small, and so shaped as to serve as anchors for a suspended back cushion if required.

They are therefore a minor portion of the design, being functional rather than merely decorative. The inner portion of the back, which is doweled to the posts, has its vertical members slightly bent to conform with the line of the vase splat which also has a slight double curve front and back. The top rail or cresting, which is pinned both to the uprights and the posts, is shaped in three dimensions. The heavy bottom rail is scooped out from the front while maintaining sufficient thickness to accept the dowels.

The back posts themselves are works of art, with compound curves and sweeping taper that turns inward at the top to merge gracefully with the central cresting. The legs are given extra weight where they receive the stretchers without distracting from their normal appearance—except from the rear—a detail that in less skillful hands might well have given the cabrioles a clumsy appearance and spoiled the whole piece. Dimensions of the daybed are: Length 68 inches, height 40 inches, width 22 inches.

LEG

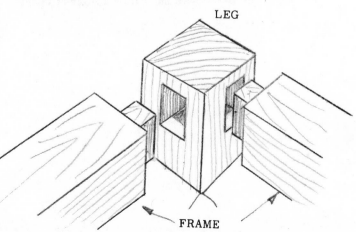

FRAME

23

PILGRIM CRADLE—1625-1675

One of the earliest pieces of joinery to turn up in this country is the oak-framed cradle shown here, which may possibly date back as far as 1625. The panels are of pine and chamfered on the inside. All joints are tenoned and pinned. The knobs are not only a relief from the general severity of this utilitarian piece, but handy for rocking and for tying on a light covering over the wings to form a hood.

As usual, the rockers are made and fitted on separately into slots cut in the bottom of the posts. They are carefully shaped to a quite flat arc so that the cradle will stand firmly upright when at rest. The sharper curve at the ends tend increasingly to bring it back into equilibrium, while the projecting toe pieces effectively check any normal danger of falling over and also provide a means of rocking the cradle comfortably with the foot. The only decoration beside the knobs is the channel molding of the top rails and center stiles.

The dimensions of this old piece are: 37 inches long, 16¼ inches wide, and 23½ inches tall.

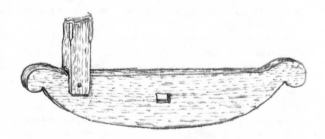

material such as leather or cloth to support the cushions or pillows.

A fair number of cradles have survived from early Colonial days. These, and many later ones, range in style from the heavy, oak-paneled variety to the suspended barrel cradle and the high-standing Windsor type which is related to the more aristocratic but far less popular rocking crib. Only a couple of the earliest, and more interesting, cradles are included here.

24

OAK CRADLE—1690

Another oak cradle, this time with pine panels and a much more ambitious design is shown here. This is supposed to have been constructed by a chest maker because the moldings are similar to those used on many chests. This point is debatable because every woodworker had a variety of molding planes and combined them to make up the molding desired. This can be seen from the variety of hollows and rounds and beads, etc., illustrated here. Nevertheless, this cradle obviously was made in the late 17th century at the height of the split-spindle craze. Some such cradles have half-spindles with the flat side turned in. This one uses flats only against the stiles in the manner of architectural engaged columns or pilasters.

The top of the cradle hood is molded at the front and back, and decorated with gouge and chisel cuts at the edges of the sides. While the rails, stiles and bottom are finished smooth and flat inside, the panels are uneven being chamfered to fit into grooves in rails and stiles without benefit of applied molding. The only molding nailed on is the coving under the overhanging top. Stiles and rails are stop-chamfered around the panels. Note that the back spindles are truncated to fit into the rails and are much less ornate than the side spindles. Surprisingly little wear is evident on this piece after more than 270 years.

This cradle is 32½ inches long, 18 inches wide, and the sides are 16¾ inches high, which is equivalent to 21½ inches from the floor. The rockers are 24 inches long, 3 inches high, and ¾ inch thick. The oak rails, grooved for decoration, are 1¼ by 3 inches. The cradle top is ⅞ inch thick, the posts 2¼ inches square, and the center stile is 3¼ inches wide.

SECTION II

Tables: Seat, Refectory, Tavern, Joint, Gateleg, Trestle, Butterfly, Hutch. Stands

There seems to be a greater variety of antique tables than almost any other piece of furniture unless it be chairs, and, of course, chair-tables have to be included under both heads. All we can hope to do here, however, is to make a sampling that will include the commoner varieties made of native woods by anonymous craftsmen.

The first tables made were probably the Pilgrim board trestles—a single board, eight feet long or more, resting loosely on a pair of trestle legs wedged so they could readily be taken apart after meals. Smaller ones may have been permanently assembled, or the top held by pins to the trestles so that it could be tilted, or removed.

Many were of the sawbuck type, wedged, and with footrests, the longer ones having an extra prop in the middle of the truss to keep the board from sagging. Various ingenious de-vices were used to keep the trestles vertical—very deep boards for trusses, or the truss board right under the top and slotted to hold the trestle legs.

Where there was room for side tables, mas-sive boards with turned legs may have been used. Even this type may have a detachable top, held in position either with dowels or by fitting the tops of the legs into recesses in the underside of the board. This long, heavy table is now often classed as the refectory type though such may never have seen the inside of a monastery, and, like the early chests were no doubt useful, on occasion, to sleep upon—or under!

As houses grew larger or had more rooms, small tables for all purposes grew popular. In the 17th century many sturdy small tables were made with turned, splayed legs like oversized joint stools. In Pennsylvania the German types might have splayed "square-turned" legs, but all had four stretchers on which to keep the feet off the cold floors.

The end of the 17th century saw a great variety of country-made tables, many decorated with fancy turned legs, stretchers, scalloped aprons, and fancy brackets. Some had high side stretchers, some medial stretchers, and some had both. Among the first drop-leaf types were the famed butterfly tables dating from about 1690. Table-chairs and table-settles, and hutch tables were all around in the early Colonial days. The original hutch was a long, narrow, side table with a cupboard be-

low, but the Pilgrim version was a small table that was also a seat and therefore had a much lower base than the original hutch.

Most so-called hutch chairs with the high box are really hutch tables. Where they have only a drawer in place of the hutch (as in the example illustrated) they are, properly, chair-tables. Many stands are of the table type; that is, they serve to support various objects on a flat upper surface, and this is the type included here, exemplified by some double-purpose pieces that illustrate the inventive skill and designing capacity of the Colonial furniture maker.

25

SIDE TABLE

This large and heavy oak table, though once used in a church, is typical of the massive side tables found in early dining halls. Only one side of the apron is carved, and the brackets were added to replace those missing. The 34¼-inch-wide top is made of two planks, 1⅜ inches thick, the end grain hidden by small cleats. It overhangs the frame by 8⅞ inches at each end. The apron is 1½ inches thick and 4 inches deep. The carving is of a well-known pattern used in the 16th century and later. It has no ecclesiastical connotation. The legs are turned from 3½-inch square stock, bringing the frame length to 71¼ inches long by 26 inches wide. The stretchers, decorated by a twin bead at the lower edge, are 3 inches high by 2¼ inches thick. The table stands 28¾ inches high.

26

JOINED STOOL-TABLE

A sturdy, joined stool such as this that can also serve as a table was a common item of furniture in houses of the late 17th century. This one is of maple, and when found its charming proportions were disguised under a coat of black paint decorated with gold striping. The top, obviously, is made extra long to serve as a table when needed. The whole piece is of maple and the turnings are especially fine. The legs are splayed both ways, and the stretcher tenons set well over and short, so as not to weaken them unduly. Note the interesting transition from the turnings to the square section. The frame at the stretchers measures 16½ × 13½ inches; the stool table is 23 inches tall (the feet being worn down at least ½ inch); the frame top 13 × 10⅝ inches; and the 1-inch-thick single-board top 23¾ × 14½ inches.

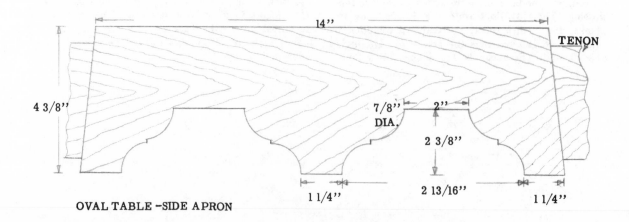

OVAL TABLE – SIDE APRON

27

JOINT TABLE

28

OVAL-TOP JOINT TABLE

Many joint tables are referred to as joint (or joined) stools, regardless of size or whether or not they incorporate a drawer. This one, 27 inches high, was most likely used for both purposes. This is a Pennsylvania table of yellow pine, made about 1750, with turned legs splayed in one direction only, thus simplifying the construction of the drawer. The top, originally in one piece, is fastened with pins into the tops of the legs. The only decoration is the beading of the aprons, the side ones being too narrow to hide the drawer runners. The legs are typical pine turnings, graceful but without any sharp arrises to break off. The feet are but little worn and the whole piece is in a remarkable state of preservation. The top measures 22¼ inches long and 14½ inches wide.

In this walnut splay-legged table are demonstrated a number of things beside the beauty of well-turned legs. The shapely aprons are set in the center of the legs instead of in the more normal flush position, thus weakening them unduly (see page 18). Furthermore, they are set into the legs their full length instead of being tenoned. The crack in the leg between the two pegs (upper right) shows the danger of driving square pegs in smaller drilled holes in brittle wood, when the pegs are exactly in line. The stretchers originally were beautifully molded, but their upper edges were reduced in thickness, so that subsequent wear is excessive. The table top is made of three boards, doweled together and pegged to the legs. As this did not provide sufficient support for the rounded outer boards, a wide (½ inch × 2½ inches) cleat was let into the tops of the side aprons, extending out almost to the edges of the boards. This also keeps the three top sections in line and deters warping—altogether a beautiful piece spoiled by careless construction sometime around 1690-1700.

The nicely shaped top measures 32½ inches by 27¾ inches maximum, and the table is 25¼ inches high. The stretchers are 1⅝ inches wide and 1 inch thick. The 1⅝-inch square legs have 12-inch long turnings. The 4⅜-inch-deep skirt is shaped as shown in the drawing.

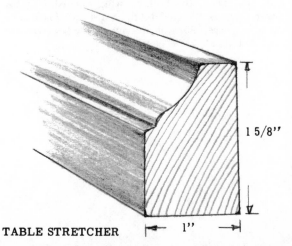

1 5/8''

1''

TABLE STRETCHER

29

HIGH-STRETCHER TABLE

More decorative than handsome, this 5-stretcher table of the "tavern" type has a pine breadboard top with wide end cleats, into which is tenoned a strip along the front edges and back that hides the cleat end grain, and forms a frame. This top is pegged into the legs which are 1½ inches square. The drawer rail is faced with an arch molding that is carried around the legs, ends, and back, effectively separating the drawer section from the somewhat crude brackets and skirts. The latter are a duplicate of the brackets, doubled at the center. The danger of pinning the bracket too close to the bottom edge is shown by the broken segment of the left hand bracket. The medial stretcher, being tenoned horizontally into the end ones, is of course pinned from the top. The ball-turned stretchers with vase centers, the ball-turned legs, and the cup feet show little signs of wear. The cotter-pinned drop handle to the drawer is correct for the period 1680-1690, as is the single-dovetail drawer which runs on slides, and has a nailed-on back, the bottom being dadoed into the front only, and nailed to the sides and back. The table measures 30½ inches by 22 inches over the top, and stands 25¾ inches high.

30

LIBRARY TABLE

Here is a fine example of a Pennsylvania-type library table in walnut of the 1700-1730 period, with an exceptionally graceful scalloped skirt. The skirt is formed as part of the front rail which is held by one pin only at each end. This skirt is carried around all four sides. As usual with this type, the table has one small and one large drawer. These are given extra distinction by the molded drawer front lip. The drawers are made with two dovetails, front and back, to each side.

The top has rounded ends and molded edges. It is made of two boards held together by butterfly patches, and is removable. The chamfered cleats, apparent replacements, are drilled through at each end but the wooden hinge pins are missing.

The heavy flush stretchers also are molded on the upper edge and carry a bead on the lower one. The leg turnings are a neat modification of an early 17th-century type—strong but not stubby.

Over-all dimensions are 48 inches long, 32½ inches wide, and 28¾ inches high.

31

HIGH-STRETCHER TABLE

Not a table to be sat down to because of the high stretchers, this little beauty is a more refined version of the table shown in Fig. 29. There is no medial stretcher, the delicate pierced brackets give it an air of lightness, and the long drawer is more formal with two pulls instead of one, while the bold lock escutcheon helps give the small brasses more importance. The overhanging oak top has a decorative edge and looks particularly good with the curly maple drawer fronts and apron. The bottom molding extending around the table below the drawers optically balances the top and unifies that section. The square portions of the pine, ball-turned legs and stretchers give the base the solidity to carry the bulk of the top unit. Over-all, the table measures 40½ inches long, 21½ inches wide, and is 26½ inches high.

32

TAVERN TABLE—MEDIAL STRETCHER TYPE

Made sometime between 1700 and 1720, this maple table has a breadboard pine top that does not do justice to it. The end cleats apparently did not prevent the top being split and another pair of cleats was nailed to the underside of the end overhang. In spite of this the unusual turnings of the legs and medial stretcher are handsome, and in keeping with the lipped drawer and stone-molded rail beneath it. The table top is pinned through into the legs which are 1⅝ inches at the front and 1¾ inches on the sides. The stretchers are of 2 × 1¾-inch stock.

The drawer has a small lip and is made with a pair of dovetails, front and back, on each side. The tops of the drawer sides are channel-grooved—a most unusual feature—and the bottom is dadoed into the front and sides.

Dimensions are: 33⅛ inches × 23⅝ inches and 26⅝ inches high.

STONE MOLD

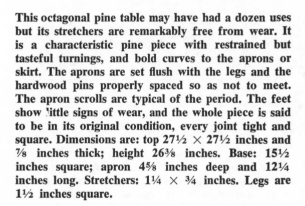

33

OCTAGONAL TABLE

34

TUCKAWAY GATELEG TABLE—1700

This octagonal pine table may have had a dozen uses but its stretchers are remarkably free from wear. It is a characteristic pine piece with restrained but tasteful turnings, and bold curves to the aprons or skirt. The aprons are set flush with the legs and the hardwood pins properly spaced so as not to meet. The apron scrolls are typical of the period. The feet show little signs of wear, and the whole piece is said to be in its original condition, every joint tight and square. Dimensions are: top 27½ × 27½ inches and ⅞ inches thick; height 26⅜ inches. Base: 15½ inches square; apron 4⅝ inches deep and 12¼ inches long. Stretchers: 1¼ × ¾ inches. Legs are 1½ inches square.

One of the smallest and neatest of occasional tables is this collapsible maple piece with three nicely turned legs, gate post, and feet. It is kept short by tilting the oval top on its narrow axis. Although it does not show in the picture, there is a heavy cleat attached by pegs to the underside of the table top. This is partially rounded on the lower side, and doweled into the tops of the fixed legs, the dowels acting as hinges. This pair of legs is connected by a wide rail, 1¼ inches thick, which is recessed at one end to receive the cutaway gateleg top when folded. The lower stretchers are almost square in section, the top corners beaded, the one connecting the fixed legs being recessed to accommodate the gate leg. The gate hinge is formed by dowels let into the upper and lower fixed stretchers. The three legs and the hinged post are 2 inches on the square, the bottom stretchers 1⅜ by 1¼ inches. The oval top measures 26¼ by 20 inches, and the over-all height is 26¼ inches. When folded, the legs and post are in line and the top vertical so that the total thickness of the table is a mere 2¾ inches.

35

TRESTLE GATELEG TABLE—1680-1700

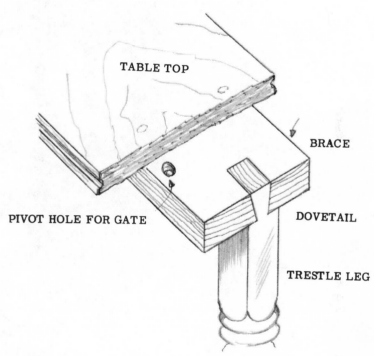

TABLE TOP

BRACE

PIVOT HOLE FOR GATE

DOVETAIL

TRESTLE LEG

In this type of gateleg table two posts take the place of four legs. These posts are provided with wide feet, and are joined together by a board tenoned into those feet. Another heavier but narrower board is dovetailed to the tops of the posts. These bottom and top boards are the anchor points for the two gates, and form, in effect, a braced trestle base for the table.

As usual with this type of construction, the gates are made of flat members tenoned together. These are 1⅝ inches wide and ¾-inch thick, with a bead down each edge for decoration. The inner stile of each gate is doweled into both the top and bottom boards, those dowels serving as hinges. The edge of the bottom board is notched to receive the gate leg when it is in the closed position.

The board forming the base is 9⅛ inches wide and ¾ inch thick, its edges also being beaded. The feet to which this board is joined are 12¾ inches long, 2½ inches wide, and 1⅞ inches thick. The legs, beautifully turned from 2⅝ inch-square stock, are tenoned to the feet. At the top end of each leg is formed a heavy dovetail that extends through the

1¼-inch-thick top board, which is 9 inches wide. This also is notched so that the gates will be flush with its edges when closed.

The central, fixed portion of the oval top is 13⅝ inches wide and 36 inches long. Each of the ⅞-inch-thick drop leaves is 16⅞ inches wide, giving the table an over-all length of 47⅜ inches. The leaves have the early style grooved joint, and are held together with butterfly hinges, still another indication of the early date at which it was made.

36

GATELEG TABLE

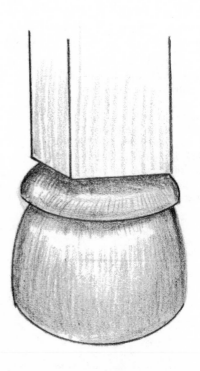

Made entirely of maple, this sturdy gateleg table has heavy but well-proportioned legs and graceful turnings. Except for those turnings no decoration is attempted. The oval top has a square edge, the leaves having tongue-and-groove joints. The center section is pegged to the fixed legs, and the deep frame is recessed to receive the split tops of the gates. The flush drawer, two-thirds the length of the frame, moves on runners instead of the old-time slides. Set in between the full thickness of the legs, it allows space for the double-thick frame made necessary by the gates. The feet were probably as shown in the sketch. Dimensions are: 52 inches long, 42 inches wide, center section 14¾ inches. Base is 13¾ by 31¾ inches; height 28½ inches.

37

CHAIR TABLE

Although dated from the last quarter of the 17th century, this chair table has a modern-looking iron rod serving as a hinge in place of the more usual pair of wooden pins—a disturbing and rawly mechanical note in an otherwise handsome piece of furniture. The one-board pine top with tapered end cleats is stiffened lengthwise by a pair of long brackets on the under edges. The large working ends of these brackets are drilled to receive the ends of the rod which also passes through the rear rounded ends of the chair arms. With the table top horizontal, the brackets fit snugly alongside the chair arms. With the top upended to form the chair back the lower table end cleat rests against the back legs. The rod then becomes an intolerable obstacle to the comfort of the sitter. The base of this contraption is made of white oak, with four sturdy turned legs extending up through the seat to form the arm posts; the shaped, square arms are tenoned to the posts. The wooden box seat is finished off with heavy molding that passes around the legs which are further tied together by aprons and stretchers. The front apron, however, is replaced by a drawer grooved to match. The chair seat is 19½ inches from the floor, and the table top is 53 inches long and 24 wide.

38

CROSS-STRETCHER CHAIR-TABLE—1777

Supposed to have originated in the Delaware Valley or lower New Jersey, this American oak chair-table is probably unique, though it has many features common to the type. It is a particularly good-looking example, almost every member has some decorative feature that fully harmonizes with the rest. An eye-catching feature is the stretcher which is half-round in section and looks heavier than its 1-inch thickness would indicate. The curved stretcher members are 1¾ inches wide, terminating in blocks 3¼ by 5¼ inches at the center junction, and 2¾ inches square on the legs. The chair feet are 4 inches in diameter and doweled into 2¼-inch-diameter leg turnings.

The seat apron is 6 inches deep on all four sides, and tenoned into the legs. The seat top is of ¾-inch oak with a thumbnail molding extending ⅜ inch beyond the legs on all four sides. In the front apron is a drawer, 10⅝ inches long and 3⅝ inches deep, which is of unusual construction. As can be seen from the picture, each side is attached to the front with a pair of wide dovetails, no attempt being made to hide them. Furthermore, the bottom is nailed on so that its end grain also shows from the front. Actually, the board ends are so smoothly finished that at first glance their end grain looks like inlay around the drawer. The drawer itself rests on runners, and it has a husky wooden knob in keeping with the other turned members. The 22-inch-long chair arms are 2¼ inches square in section, and strongly tenoned to the front and back posts, both ends being nicely rounded off, and the rear pair being drilled to receive the hinge pins that hold the top.

The top itself is in two pieces and delicately scrolled. Over-all, it measures 34½ by 27½ inches, and is strongly reinforced by a pair of cleats the full width of the two boards. The cleats are a full inch thick, with rounded and chamfered ends, and only 2 inches wide. The seat is 23¾ inches wide and 18¼ inches deep.

X-STRETCHER CHAIR-TABLE

PEDESTAL BOSS

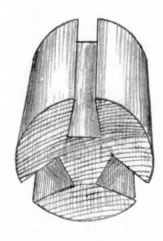

39

URN STAND—1790

Stands such as this need to be quite sturdy, with plenty of leg span so that they can support heavy and sometimes dangerous objects such as a large urn, spirit kettle (or even a samovar!), without fear of tipping. This is a good example of how such solidity can be achieved without loss of proportion or deterioration in appearance. The massive post allows of three legs, ⅞ inch thick, being dovetailed solidly into the 3¼-inch-diameter cylindrical portion at its lower end. The 3½-inch-long tails being ample to afford maximum rigidity to the widely splayed legs. These extend outward ten inches from the post center—1½ inches beyond the edge of the top which is 17 inches in diameter. This round top is carried on a tapered cleat 15½ inches long and 3½ inches wide. At this center where it is doweled to the heavy post turning this cleat is ¾ in. thick, and is reduced to ¼ inch at the ends. Six screws hold it to the top. The stand, which is all of pine, is 28⅜ inches high, with legs ⅞ inch thick and 1 inch wide where they rest on the floor.

DOVETAIL

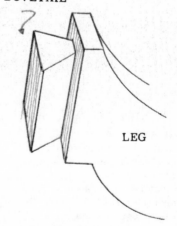

LEG

LEG DETAIL

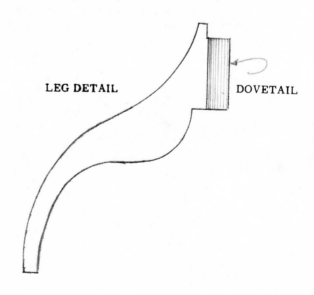

DOVETAIL

40

TILT-TOP TABLE—1790

This attractive cherry piece has the scalloped top of an earlier design that both tilts and turns without benefit of a birdcage. Instead, there is a heavy block, 1½ inches thick and 6 inches square, mounted on a 1½-inch-diameter dowel, or spindle, formed on the pedestal shaft which is 2¾ inches in diameter at that point. The revolving block has one-inch-long dowels turned on it at one edge, and on these the top tilts 90 degrees. These dowels are held to the top by blind holes drilled in a pair of long cleats. These 1¼-inch-thick cleats are screwed to the underside of the ¾-inch-thick top, lengthwise with the grain. When the top is horizontal it is held in position by the usual small brass catch hooking into a keeper let into the edge of the tilt-block.

The table top is 26 inches long, 20 inches wide, and stands 28 inches from the floor. The legs are held to the shaft by dovetails 2⅞ inches long. The bottom of the turning, and the dovetails, are covered by a flange turning incorporating a ball ornament, 1½ inches in diameter, that adds a decorative touch. This turning takes the place of the more usual metal plate intended to keep the dovetails from sliding down out of their sockets when the table is lifted. The three legs are arched upward a total distance of 10¼ inches from the floor.

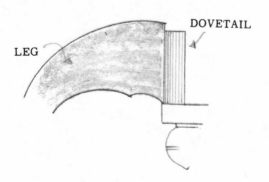

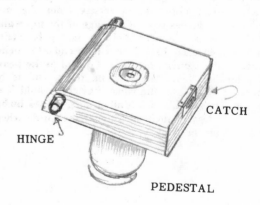

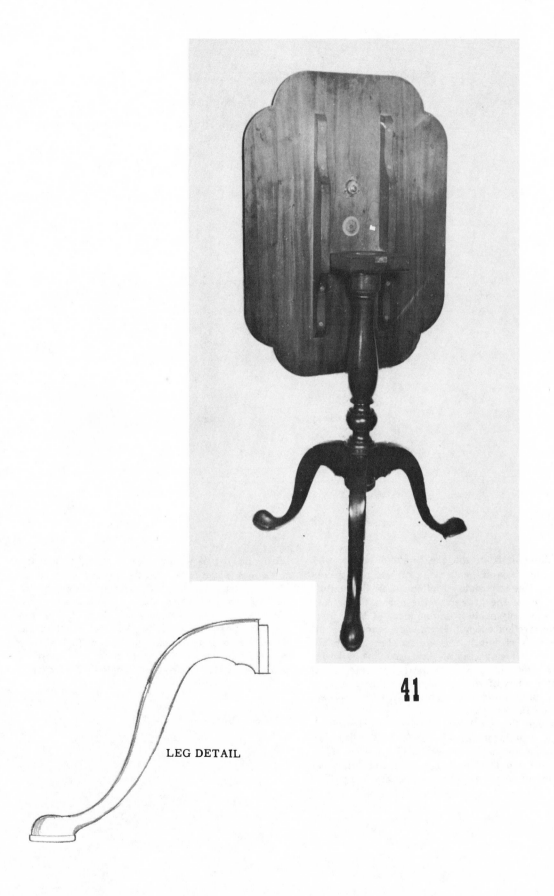

41

LEG DETAIL

42

PINE LAMP STAND—1795

Quite different from the earlier stand is this pine piece which is both smaller and of less robust construction. One important variation lies in the method used to house the drawer in the apron. This front apron is actually made from one piece of board with its center section cut out. Extra-wide tenons are cut on the ends of this board—as can be seen in the picture from the spacing of the pegs—but even this was not sufficient to prevent the board cracking at all four corners of the opening. The drawer is carried on runners and guides attached to the legs and aprons on the two sides.

Although this piece is attractive in proportions, finish, and grain, it has other defects. The legs are too slender for soft pine and tend to warp. It is also rather too light in weight to stand firmly on the floor, or to solidly support a heavy lamp. The drawer has two large dovetails at the front and two small ones at the back, and the bottom is nailed on. At some time the original peg-type knob was replaced by the present shouldered, flat Victorian type, otherwise the piece seems quite original. The top, which has a square edge, is 14 inches in width and depth, the apron is 4 inches deep, and the legs taper from 1⅛ inches at the apron level to a mere ¾ inch at the foot. The over-all height is 27 inches.

DRAWER APRON

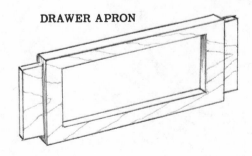

43

MAPLE LAMP STAND—1810

Less delicate, and physically heavier, lamp or candle stands were made in large numbers during the first half of the 19th century. The one illustrated here is of this more sturdy type with substantial legs and a close-fitting top dating to the late Federal period and with hardware to prove it. It is 28⅝ inches high, with a top 19⅞ inches wide by 17¼ inches deep overlapping the base ½ inch all around. The legs are 1½ inches square down to below the drawer rail, then taper, on two adjacent sides, to 1 inch at the bottom. The drawer is the full width from leg to leg, 15½ inches long and 3¼ inches high, held between stub-tenoned rails, ⅞ inch broad, above and below. The other three sides have aprons 5 inches deep to match. The drawer itself is made with the modern style multiple tenons, and a flat-cut bottom fitting into side and front grooves. On the front is a 1½-inch brass knob with a rosette and held by a post and nut—a type popular between 1790 and 1840.

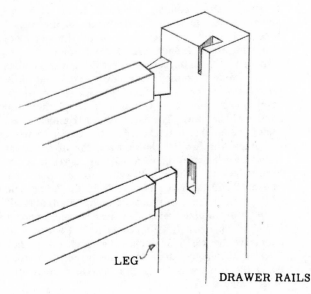

LEG

DRAWER RAILS

44

CANDLE STAND

45

CROSS-BASE STAND

So utilitarian a piece as this screw-type candle stand needs careful designing not to appear wholly mechanical. In this example the maker has actually demonstrated that a screw thread—even several of them—can be a decorative feature. In making the threaded center column, even the lower end was given a thread to simplify attachment to the turned base and incidentally enable it to be disassembled. Only the candle holders are of metal, and they are provided with thumbscrews for raising the candles in the holders as they burn down. The neat little knobs on the candle bracket provide a means of turning it on the screw without risk of splashing the hand with hot wax. The large turned rimmed table under the bracket is thickened at the center to work on several threads. The bottom and top of the main support are finished off with delicate curves that are harmonious with the spindle-type legs. All parts are of maple and the piece was made in the latter half of the 18th century. In stands 35 inches high, over-all —the foot turning being 1¾ inches thick and 6 inches in diameter. The lipped table is 14 inches in diameter; the legs 10½ inches long and 1⅛ inches thick at the largest diameter. The turned arm that holds the candles is 16 inches long and made out of 1¾-inch stock.

A well-made example of the earliest type of stand, this happily combines the medieval pattern of cross base with a turned column and an equally sturdy circular top of small diameter. The cleat that holds the top matches the thickness of the post to which it is tenoned and pinned. Nails through the thin ends of the cleat hold the top in place. The base of the column forms a dowel that passes through the feet where it is wedged. Note that the feet are undercut so that the stand rests on its toes. Dimensions of this all-walnut piece are: Top 12½ inches in diameter and 1 inch thick, standing 27 inches high. The top cleat is 2¾ inches thick and 1⅝ inches wide. The feet are 14 inches long, 2⅜ inches wide, and 2 inches thick. The turned post is 1⅝ inches in diameter.

SECTION III

Boxes, Racks, Miniature Cupboards,
Miniature Chests

From the 17th century on, a great many wooden boxes were made for a wide variety of purposes—to keep the mice away from the tallow candles, to display the family's collection of pewter spoons while hiding the knives, to hold the precious supply of salt, and so on. There were table boxes and wall boxes, lidless or lidded, and in many instances it would be quite impossible today to determine their original use and purpose. What we *do* know is that not every flat-topped table box is a Bible box, and not every slant-top box is a desk box. Some book boxes undoubtedly had a slant-top—and even a ledge at the bottom—for convenience in reading; the books being heavy and the light poor. Today such boxes are probably interesting only in proportion to the excellence of workmanship that went into them; the type of decoration—carved, incised, applied, or painted—and also the hardware

(locks, hasps, hinges, etc.). Rarely are any two alike.

In most instances, as the following examples show, these boxes were nailed together, with an occasional piece of framing or dovetailing. Many woods were used, though pine predominated for the lids of the larger boxes and for the carcases of practically all kitchen pieces. The rectangular table boxes usually have lids stiffened against warping by a pair of cleats so that they overhang an inch or more at each end. Most of the lids also overhang at the front about the thickness of the wood—or did so until they were worn down—a convenience in opening them. The earlier ones normally will be of oak, sometimes with pine lids, backs, and bottoms. All-pine boxes are usually later (or homemade), and some of them are splendidly carved all over, the soft wood being an invitation to whittling. Quite

71

often the smaller boxes—especially those made to hang—rely for their appeal on fanciful shapes.

The same observations apply to the tiny wall cupboards, cabinets, and racks—plain, painted, or elaborately carved all over. Both footed and hanging cabinets with glazed fronts were made for the display of china, pewter, or glassware. Similar ones with a solid door, paneled or plain, served for the storage of silver, small utensils, bottled medicines or stimulants, and so on. Those consisting of anywhere from two to a dozen small drawers were possibly for spices, while the stepped type would seem more adapted to bedroom use.

Racks were used principally for spoons, some incorporating a box for cutlery. Many of the more elaborate ones were undoubtedly made by skilled craftsmen; others were obviously homemade. Nevertheless they may be well worth owning and even copying.

Whether professional products or otherwise, the boxes are put together in a variety of ways that have little to do with the dating. Lid hinges vary from the pin type and leather straps to dowels or even butts applied flat, and at least one ingenious craftsman used H hinges between door and stile with only the back showing in the modern butt-hinge manner. Decoration, likewise, varies from simple chisel carving or scratching to painted designs. Even quite carefully made pieces may be held together by very obvious nails, or they may be neatly dovetailed, and it is astonishing how decorative the old handmade nail heads can be when properly applied.

46

TABLE BOX—1670

Dated 1670, this oak box, deeply carved on three sides, closely follows an old English pattern sometimes called "blind arcading." The sides are let into and nailed from the front, the front corners being gouged to help disguise the end grain—another common practice. Although the lid has an end overhang, cotter-pin hinges are used, clinched into the top of the lid. The overhang allows for cleats to help stiffen the lid, and keep it from warping. The front and sides of the lid are finished with a thumbnail molding, the front being worn almost flush with the face of the box and detracting from its appearance. The base of the box carries a heavy mitred molding of a medieval type that is exactly suited to the carving. Incidentally, the original guide lines for the carved arches are still visible. Overall dimensions of the box are: 27 inches × 19 × 11¼ inches high.

BASE MOLDING

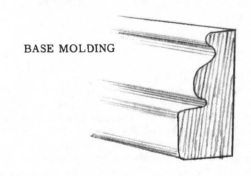

47

TABLE BOX—1677

One of the plainest and simplest of its type, this oak table box dated 1677 is an unusually interesting survival. Its lid has the normal end overhang but no cleats. As if to diminish the effect of that overhang the lid is given a wide chamfer so that it appears quite thin at the edges. Both front and back are rabbeted into the ends, the front corners being notch-carved. The bottom is simply nailed on. Cotter-pin-type hinges are used, clinched into the top face and back. The decoration is carefully executed scratch carving evidently done with the joiner's scriber. The box is 22¼ inches long, over-all, 17½ inches deep, and 9 inches high.

48

OAK DESK BOX—1690

The simplest of slant-top boxes is this oak piece dated from 1690, its top decorated with a delightful pair of butterfly hinges. The two sections of the top are quite heavy, the side and front edges have an overlapping thumbnail molding. The box front is dadoed to receive the ends which are secured by a couple of heavy nails at each corner.

The bottom is nailed on and its edges are covered with a heavy cove molding 1¾ inches deep. At one time there was a lock, but the battered keyhole is now covered with a sheet of tin held on by six nails of a later vintage than the box. Inside, the box has three drawers raised 3¾ inches from the bottom. The thin partitions and the bottom strip that holds them are dadoed together and into the box top and ends. The drawers are quite crudely put together with nails—possibly as later substitutes for the original pigeonholes. This box is 22½ inches long, 10 inches high at the back, 7 inches high at the front, and is 19 inches deep.

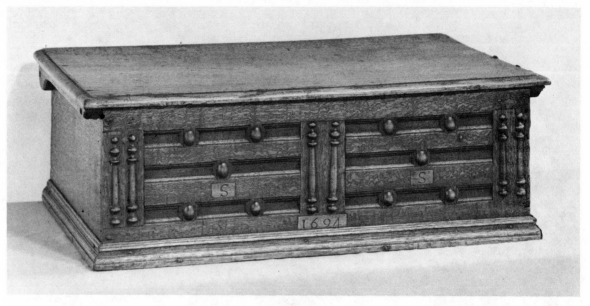

49

TABLE BOX—1694

In this box, dating from 1694, we have an excellent example of both careful construction and restrained decoration. For once the split spindles and bosses have not been ebonized to dominate the whole pattern, and there are not too many of them. The entire box is of oak, with a molded lid reinforced by sturdy cleats that also serve as hinges. Both back and front boards are halved into the sides and they, together with the base molding are held together by nails, no attempt being made to hide the nail heads.

The panels were made by routing out the thick front board to form on it what appear to be the four rails. These rails were given grooved and chamfered edges to produce the effect of panel molding. Next, the large end and center stiles, made separately, were pinned in place. Then the little panel stiles were molded, their ends shaped to fit over the molding on the rails, and nailed down. Finally the split bosses and spindles applied on top of the stiles. The finishing touch was the letting into the oak surface of the small pine blocks bearing the initials and

date. These are about ⅜ inch thick. The base molding, as the picture shows, was mitered then nailed on last of all.

The over-all dimensions of this box are: 28 inches by 17¾, by 10 inches high.

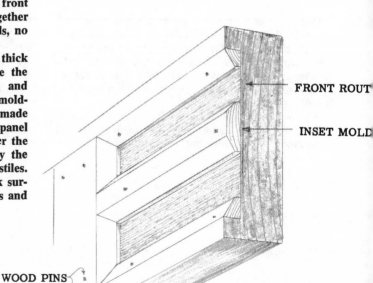

FRONT ROUT

INSET MOLD

WOOD PINS

50

TABLE BOX

One of the neatest—and simplest—table boxes ever designed is this highly finished oak piece dated well before 1700. The box is of nice proportions, smooth-surfaced, with a deep base molding. The lid, lightened by a thumbnail molding, extends over the pair of cleats through which pegs pass to form hinges. The sole applied decoration consists of split spindles and bosses of maple, flanking a small panel for the owner's initials. This is a vast improvement over the then popular combination of spindles and bosses on molded and carved panels. The front and back are rabbeted to receive the ends; the joints nailed. The box is 29½ inches long, 17¼ inches deep, and 9 inches high.

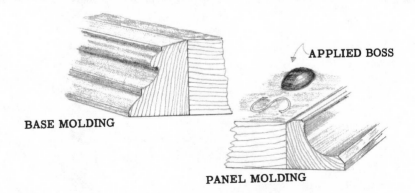

BASE MOLDING

APPLIED BOSS

PANEL MOLDING

51

DESK BOX—1792

A desk box of this sort needs only a hole through the back of its cresting to become a wall box—perhaps for candles, with flint, steel, or tinder in the drawer. In either position it is attractive in polished maple, chisel-carved, and lettered by an expert. The ⅝-inch-thick lid is held by cotter-pin hinges clinched through the underside of the lid, the latter overlapping the sides slightly, with the bottom edge nicely rounded. The bottom is fastened to the ends with dovetails arranged to hold the sides together but useless for holding the bottom on. The sides also are dadoed to receive the inner box bottom. The ⅞-inch-thick base is nailed on to the sides and bottom.

The drawer is somewhat battered, sliding on a much-worn bottom. It has a tiny lip, almost worn away, and has one front dovetail with the front and sides dadoed to receive the bottom. The box front over the drawer is rabbeted and nailed on flush with the lower front edge of the sides. The drawer knob is brass. Originally, the old nailheads must have been much more decorative than they are today.

The most professional thing about the box is the carving and lettering, the latter being in a delightful script with flourishes. The date, as shown on the lid, is 1792. Dimensions are: 14¼ inches long, 8¼ inches deep, and 19 inches over the back.

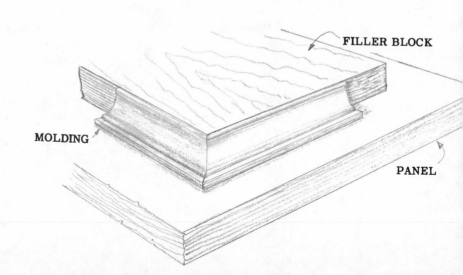

FILLER BLOCK

MOLDING

PANEL

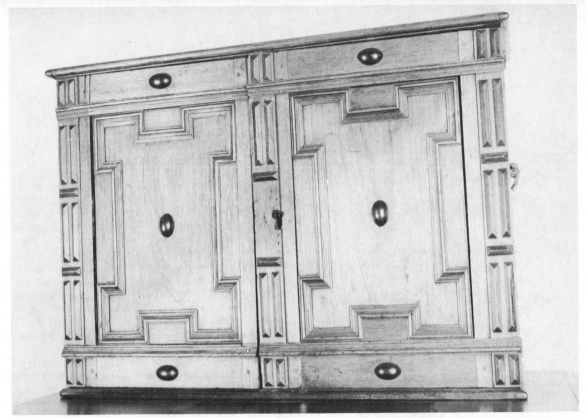

52

TABLE CABINET

Probably made as a seagoing or traveling secretary, this small cabinet-a mere 23 inches high-with drop handles at each end, is a charming piece of late 17th-century cabinetry. It is also ingenious. There are two doors, but the right-hand one incorporates what appears to be a central stile, acting as a closing jamb for both doors. Inside there are seven drawers, and an eighth that seems to be an afterthought as it is entirely devoid of moldings. This leaves seven pigeonholes of ¼-inch material dadoed together, for additional storage. The drawers are simply made, with a single dovetail, and the bottom nailed on. The cabinet back, rough and plain, also is nailed on. On the right-hand door there is a substantial lock which has an additional catch that engages with a heavy iron hook attached to the central shelf—a corner of one drawer being cut away to accommodate it.

This cabinet is made entirely of oak, except for the drawers and dividers, and the attached decorations. The hinges are an unusually decorative combination of butterfly and strap pattern, with the strap portion on the inside of the door. The doors, which are a full inch thick, are grooved for rectangular panels. On the exterior, these panels have applied frame moldings and filler blocks to give them a geometric, eared shape. The stiles, door bottoms, and top rails have applied, triangular-section moldings, and a half dozen ebonized, oval bosses supply the necessary accents. The cabinet is 31⅝ inches long, 12 inches deep, and 23 inches high.

DUMMY STILE

INTERIOR VIEW FIG. 52

53

MINIATURE SPICE CABINET

This small cabinet with its oversized hardware was made in Pennsylvania in the early 1700s and is all walnut. Such small pieces were often used as silver cabinets or for the storage of jewelry or similar small items of value. Even in a well-proportioned piece such as this, the tendency seems to have been to use too-heavy moldings as in the crown and base moldings here. Otherwise the design is good and the trumpet-type leg turnings and stretchers are exquisite. The chased hinges and keyhole escutcheons (one of which adorns a dummy keyhole) are finely made though slightly oversize. The knobs are excellent.

The pattern of this cabinet is an advanced type of early 18th-century style with an extra-deep base and tall drawers at the sides. The double-arch molds of the apron are not common, even on lowboys, and a six-legged lowboy (which this base by itself would constitute) would be a rarity in any case.

Though small, this piece is made of comparatively thick wood, except for the nosing over the legs and the strips used to form the beads applied to the ogee curves. The pattern of the stretchers follows that of the apron. The base cabinet sides are dovetailed together, the molding mitered on leaving a slight recess on top of the cabinet sides into which the narrower and shallower upper unit is set. The cabinet doors are strongly made with through tenons, wide stiles and rails, and raised panels of good proportions. The meeting stiles are rabbeted, the right-hand one given a decorative bead. The heavy crown molding finishes under a widely overhanging but thin board top. This molding is thick enough at the bottom to leave a little overhang at the front when the doors are closed. Measurements are: 16¼ inches wide, 34½ inches tall, and 8⅝ inches deep.

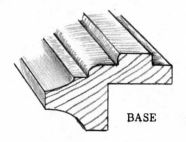

BASE

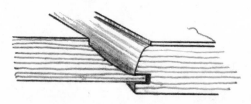

PANEL

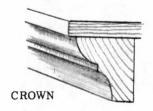

CROWN

HINGE

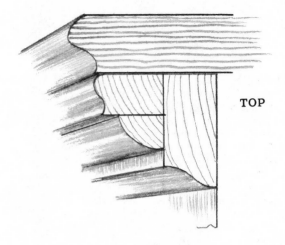

TOP

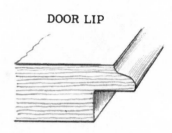

DOOR LIP

54

HANGING CUPBOARD—1725-1750

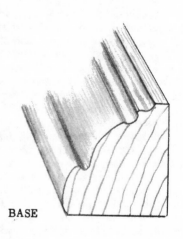

BASE

PANEL

This sturdily built walnut cupboard hails from Pennsylvania and is intended either to stand on a table or hang on a wall. The front stiles and rails are tenoned together, with the sides set in and pinned from the front. The back also is inset and the base molding is mitered and nailed through into the bottom on the front and ends. The crown molding is built up of several seemingly unrelated pieces. There is, however, a deep molding, flat on the face but with an ogee-formed lower edge, nailed to the case. On top of this is another mitered strip with a reverse ogee, the angle being filled with a quarter-round. Above all is the cabinet top, its ends and front edge shaped in another and more pronounced ogee, the whole sadly battered and worn.

Strangely enough for such a rugged piece, the cupboard door is nicely lipped, and considerable work has been done on the panel, the fielded portion being given a molded edge, details of which are sketched. The eye-catchers on this piece, however, are the scroll hinges, which need no description. Over-all, this cupboard measures: Height 27¼ inches, width 25¼ inches, depth 18 inches.

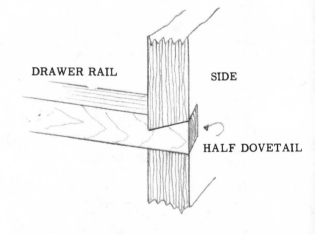

DRAWER RAIL   SIDE

HALF DOVETAIL

55

PINE TABLE CUPBOARD—18TH CENTURY

Simply designed and neatly put together is this tall, slender pine cupboard intended to be placed on a table or shelf. The door in particular is exceedingly well made, with a thick, raised panel, and nice proportions, plus a double-pinned frame hanging on three small dovetail hinges. There are two special features to be noted—one being the fact that the door stiles are let into the edges of the sides above the drawer section. Below that point, alongside the drawers, the edges of the sides are visible. Into these are sunk the ends of the rails separating the drawers where they are held by half-dovetail joints that also are visible.

The bottom of the cupboard section is a ¾-inch board notched to receive the door-frame stiles so that it is flush with them. This is held by nails through the sides and front. The top is given a similar appearance by the insertion of a rail between the stiles. This is partly covered by a cove molding over which the overhanging top board is nailed. To the edge of this thick top board is nailed ¾-inch, half-round molding—a rather heavy-handed touch.

In the lower section the drawers are lipped, the lips given a slight ogee section. The drawer sides are held with a single dovetail, and the bottoms have tapered edges so that they can be set into grooves on all four sides in the manner of panels. Heavy and crude partitions have been installed inside the drawers, evidently long after the drawers were made. The drawers also are graduated in size—4, 5, and 6 inches deep respectively.

Inside the cupboard there is nothing but three rough shelves. The back of the entire piece consists of an unsmoothed board ⅞ inch thick, nailed on. This and several other rough-and-ready features mentioned suggest later additions and alterations by some unskilled or careless person to what was originally an attractive and well-made cabinet.

This piece is 47 inches high, 18¾ inches wide. The door measures 27 by 9⅝ inches, and the drawer fronts are 16¼ inches long. The heavy base molding is 1⅛ by 1⅛; the crown molding is 1¼ inches thick and 1¾ inches wide, including the top. Details are shown in the sketches.

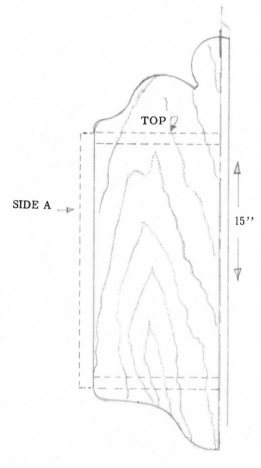

TOP

SIDE A

15''

56
KEY CUPBOARD

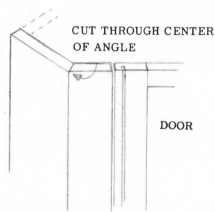

CUT THROUGH CENTER
OF ANGLE

DOOR

Here is one key cupboard whose design is an improvement on the painted decoration. Small butterfly or H hinges also would have helped. Nevertheless it is an appealing piece, countrymade around 1800, and probably decorated by the owner. The door is carefully made with tenoned joints, and grooved to receive the panel. The edge beads help to break up the flat front. The sides are made of two pieces carefully joined and glued at the correct angle. They are secret-nailed to the ends of the back pieces and the top and bottom. Over-all, this is 15 inches high, 8¼ inches wide, and 5½ inches deep, measured into the angle, and is of course all pine.

57

FISHTAIL PIPE BOX

This somewhat crude specimen of a well-known pattern of hanging pipe box is of pine and stands 17½ inches high, the box section being 7 inches deep—enough to support the long stem of a church-warden clay pipe. The little tobacco drawer below has a shouldered front, with a flush back and inset bottom, all nailed together with square, bradlike nails. The knob is a simple tapered peg driven tightly in. The front of the box is ⅜ inch thick, rabbeted to the sides. The back, which shows the marks of a round-nose plane, is set between the sides and shouldered over them at the top. A chamfered base is nailed on. It appears to date from the late 18th century. Dimensions are: 17½ inches high, 4¾ inches wide, 3⅞ inches deep. Drawer front is 2½ inches high, box front stands 9¾ inches maximum from the base.

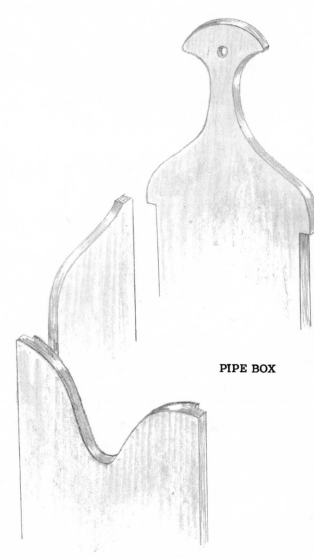

PIPE BOX

58

SPOON RACKS—1740-1750

59

MINIATURE CHEST—1710

Here are three Dutch or Pennsylvania German spoon racks. The left- and right-hand ones are from New Jersey, one deeply chisel-carved in the lower sections and with more delicate tracery in a tulip design above. The other has both scratch carving and painted designs all over it. In both pieces the edges of the front strips also are decorated, and both racks have fancy wheel-motif crestings. Rectangular slots are provided to receive the spoons which must be inserted from the top.

The central spoon rack, from Pennsylvania, is heavily carved with both wheel and geometric designs, plus three cut-out "tassels" on the bottom as though it was intended to represent some fabric. This piece has the spoon shelves nailed on from the front, the others from the back. Only one of its shelves is decorated.

The left-hand rack measures 18¾ inches up to the shoulder, and 21½ inches over-all, and is 9¾ inches wide. The shelves are six inches apart, starting 6 inches from the bottom. The center rack is 24½ inches tall, 9 inches wide, and the third one 24 by 9½ inches—18 inches to the shoulders.

Painted Indian red, this simple, well-proportioned small chest has excellent ball feet and is innocent of any decoration beyond the double-arch molding arranged across the front and mitered into vertical end strips as if to represent drawers, plus ogee molding under the lid. The upper arch molding is notched at the center for a keyhole escutcheon now missing. The top is a single board ½ inch thick. In the absence of cleats it has warped sufficiently to displace the end sections of the crown molding. The hinges are of the cotter-pin type. Nails clinched on the outside hold a large lock in place. While there is no evidence of there having been a base molding at the front, the bevelled ends of the bottom board suggest they may once have been covered. Made wholly of poplar, the chest is nailed together, the sides being rabbeted into the front and back, with the bottom inset and nailed. The dimensions are 21½ inches wide, 13 inches deep, and it stands 14 inches high including the feet.

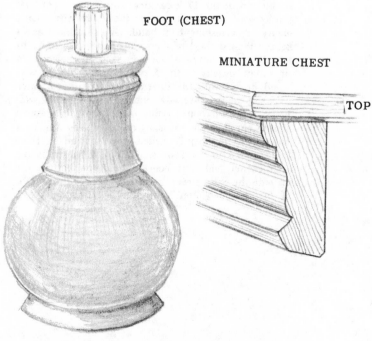

FOOT (CHEST)

MINIATURE CHEST

TOP

60

LIQUOR CHEST—1800

Transporting your own cellar was a serious problem at the end of the 17th century, and many a country gentleman took pains to ensure that there was always plenty of refreshment on hand. One solution was to keep a locked chest of spirits on hand, especially in traveling, and quite a number of such chests turn up today, usually in the form of tool chests or firewood boxes, with the internal parts removed. Such a box is shown here—a pine piece complete with lock, and well bound with iron straps. Like most simple chests it has the ends rabbeted into the front and back, and firmly nailed, the bottom, in turn, being nailed to the four sides. Two iron straps on each corner and four bent to hold the bottom on provide the extra strength needed to carry the weight of fifteen half-gallon bottles of heavy green glass.

These bottles are square and tapered so that they fit the compartments snugly. The large lock is riveted on from the inside, and a fancy iron escutcheon surrounds the keyhole. At each end is a wrought-iron drop handle anchored by a pair of heavy cotters clinched on the inside of the box.

All wood is of full 1-inch thickness, including the lid, which is finished off with a simple applied molding. The hinges are of the double strap chest type, offset to fasten inside the back. The interior of the box is, or was, fitted with partitions forming fifteen cells each of which held a bottle—three rows of five bottles each. The partitions were made of ¼-inch whitewood, housed into all four sides and the bottom, but not otherwise fastened. The dimensions over the box body are: 25½ by 16, by 13½ inches high.

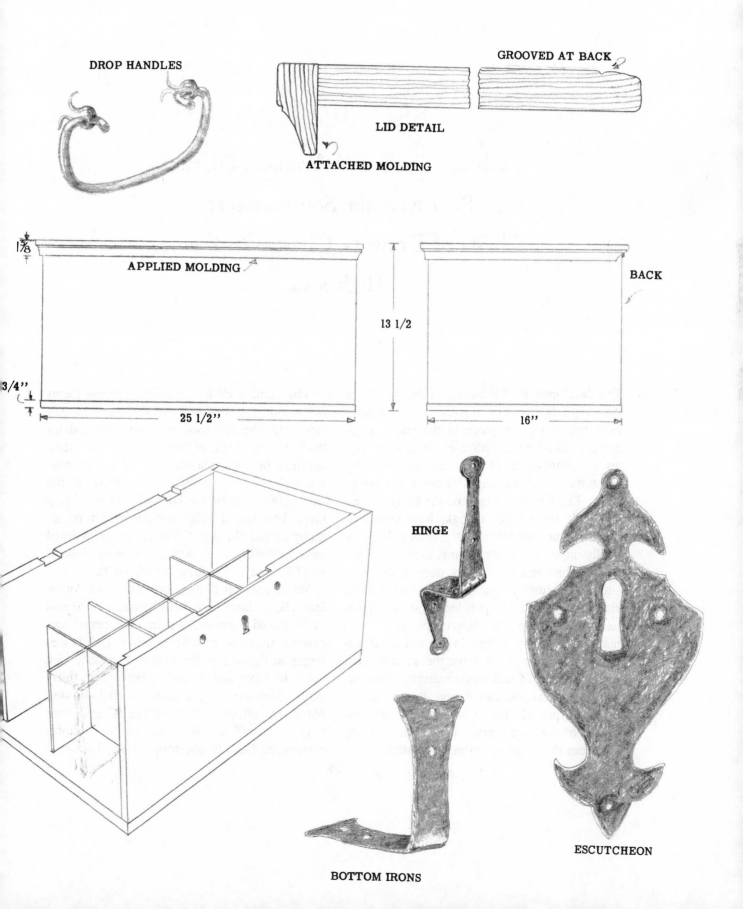

DROP HANDLES

GROOVED AT BACK

LID DETAIL

ATTACHED MOLDING

1 7/8

APPLIED MOLDING

BACK

13 1/2

3/4"

25 1/2"

16"

HINGE

BOTTOM IRONS

ESCUTCHEON

SECTION IV

Chests: Six-Board, Framed, Pilgrim, Pennsylvania, Southwestern, Chests of Drawers, Chests On Frames, Highboys.

The development of the chest of drawers from the simple box is easy to trace in this section. However, not every piece in the series originated in this country. Most of them were copies or adaptations of originals imported by colonists at various stages of the early settlement. The fact that many of the early pieces, especially those made of oak, were commonplace in the mother country makes it practically impossible to determine, unless they are dated, when and where they were made. This situation is further confused because the more elaborate framed and paneled chests are likely to be older than the plainer box-type pieces made for country people in the scattered settlements. However, it must be remembered that the dating of antiques is scarcely a science, and, as far as we can expect to find them, certain types of decorative patterns are repeated over a long period of time, on a variety of pieces that may not even be related.

The chest itself is one of the earliest forms of furniture, and the paneled variety, which represents the best form of construction, dates back to the 15th century. Some decorative carvings of these chests, such as the lunette, the arch, and the guilloche, so popular in the mid-1700s, can be traced back almost a century. The famed tulip pattern found on so many carved chests in Connecticut and painted ones in Pennsylvania was common in Holland in 1639 and in England before 1660.

While painted designs are found on American chests dated anywhere between 1690 and 1850, the widespread American manner of decorating them with split spindles and bosses begun at the end of the 17th century does not seem to have lasted more than about thirty years. This use of split turnings on both simple board chests and elaborate framed ones may very well be attributed to the country craftsman. Here is one form of applied orna-

88

ment that needs little skill to make, so long as a lathe is available; a decorative idea that certainly would appeal to the worker in wood, who was not familiar with the art of carving. The same search for a method of quick and easy adornment is seen in the use of applied moldings, especially in the very heavy ones projecting well above the panel surface. These, so often used on English pieces in the middle 1600s, produced a rugged architectural effect, yet called for no more than simple mitering. Both of these decorative forms date in America from the late 17th century, and indeed are often used together as will be seen in **Fig. 63.**

Of the two contrasting highboys included in this section, the first is no more than a chest of drawers on a low frame which also incorporates a drawer. The other has only four legs with no stretcher, and four drawers in the base so that it is far less substantial both in appearance and in fact. Many of these pieces have six legs, often with a tall base that is, in effect, a lowboy and made separately. When the base has several layers of drawers, the bottommost coming within a few inches of the floor, the piece is called a chest-on-chest.

61

PILGRIM CHEST—1640-1670

This splendidly carved chest is reputed to be the work of a Pilgrim coffinmaker named Winslow. The all-over carving of the front may have been the inspiration for the later, and inferior, Hadley and similar styles with flat and shallow-cut designs. This Pilgrim chest carving incorporates the arch motif common on 16th-century English chests with the stylized tulip and clover patterns so widely adopted in this country. The scroll pattern on the bottom rail is one variation of a somewhat older design. The chest is wholly of oak, with twin-paneled ends, the rails being groove molded in the then current fashion. The front legs are 3¾ inches wide and 1⅜ inches thick so that there is plenty of material to hold the rail tenons, both front and side. As usual, the short panel stiles have molded edges. The rails, top and bottom, are chamfered as are the legs where they are grooved to receive the panels. The top of this chest is in one piece, with a wide thumbnail molding, the ends accommodating a pair of 1⅛-inch-thick cleats. Hinges are of the cotter-pin type. The bottom rail is 5¾ inches from the floor, and the chest top 27¾ inches up. The top measures 47⅜ by 21¾ inches.

62

PINE BLANKET CHEST—1700

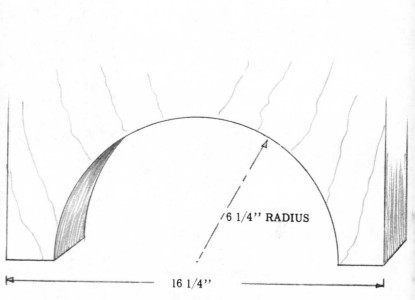

6 1/4'' RADIUS

16 1/4''

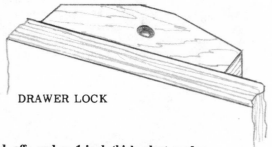

DRAWER LOCK

Chests of this type, with dummy drawers, are common, some of them having heavy ball feet at the front. Although a single-drawer chest with a lid top, it is made to look more important—and a more decorative piece than it is—by dressing it up with single-arch molding, keyhole escutcheons, and tear-drop handles.

The false upper drawers provide a storage space under the lid 14 inches deep. The bottom drawer, under the floor of the chest portion, is 8 inches deep, and the base molding beneath it is 8 inches from the floor.

An interesting detail is the method used to lock the drawer. At top center, behind the drawer front, is nailed a triangular block of wood (see sketch) with a 3/16-inch hole drilled through it. When the drawer is closed, this hole is exactly under another hole in the chest bottom. A short iron rod pushed down through the top hole enters the hole in the block, preventing the drawer from being opened. What happens when the chest is packed with clothing, etc., is best left to the imagination.

From below the lid to the top of the drawer, the front edges of the sides are cut back to receive the front panel. This brings the panel into line with the drawer front when the drawer is closed. The panel is therefore nailed into the edges of the end boards, and the nails covered with the molding. The lid, as usual, is of one board, 38 by 16¼ inches, with the edges rounded off, and a 1-inch-thick cleat under each end. The feet are formed by cutting out a semicircle with a radius of 6¼ inches from the bottom of the end boards. The back of the chest is nailed to the edges of the ends and base. Over-all dimensions are: 38 inches wide, 16¼ inches deep, and 32½ inches high.

63

PANELLED CHEST—1680

Strongly molded chests such as this, with heavy geometric panel decorations take more kindly to spindle ornaments because they tend to subdue them. In this paneled pine chest from Massachusetts even the molding in high-relief is not overdone, and the heavy blocks beneath the lid—a conceit often indulged in on Cromwellian forms and 16th-century cupboards—add a note of simplicity while balancing the sturdy feet and forming a logical termination to the four stiles. Altogether this is a satisfying design, rugged yet balanced. The spindles and rods are of maple. The framed lid has lost its front section so that the end tenons are seen. The top is extended at both front and ends to match the heavy moldings above and below the drawer. All three drawer panels are framed with applied molding so that they provide the same sunken-panel effect as the built-up moldings of the chest section. The chest end panels are recessed and flat. This piece dates from around 1680, and its dimensions are: Length 47 inches, depth 20¼ inches, and height 27¾ inches.

64

DECORATED PINE CHEST—1790-1820

Here is a six-board pine chest, nailed together, the ends inset into dadoes in front and back, and extended down to form legs with a simple, straight saw-cut dividing the feet. The ¾-inch-thick, single-board lid has plain back and front edges, only the ends having thumb moldings, with two flat cleats outside the ends, and, inside, a pair of strap-type chest hinges. The finish of the boards is far from smooth, rough-sawn inside and bearing the marks of an old-time round-nosed plane on the outside—all of which suggests that the elaborate decoration was added much later, probably during the first half of the 19th century. At that time the whole chest was painted, and the designs stenciled on the large, single-board front in gold, white, yellow, red, and dark brown, on a background of dead black.

The boards are an inch thick and the pine soft as is indicated by the large number of nails used to hold the joints—a strictly utilitarian piece originally, made attractive with sophisticated decoration of a quality far superior to the woodworker's craftsmanship. This piece is quite large, standing 29 inches high over-all, by 48¾ inches long, and 20¾ inches from back to front. The legs raise its bottom 5 inches from the floor.

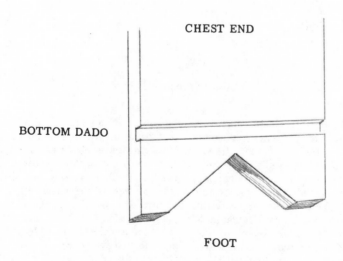

CHEST END

BOTTOM DADO

FOOT

65

BLANKET CHEST—1735

The makers of this simple, box-type chest went to a great deal of trouble to disguise it as a handsome piece of furniture. Of the three apparent drawer fronts, only one—the bottom one—is real in spite of the extra pulls and lock plate or key escutcheon. The whole thing is of pine, with the edges of the end boards fully exposed. These boards extend down to form legs, each board having a semicircular cut-out extending as high as the bottom board of the chest. Marking the horizontal divisions between the drawers are half-round moldings terminating inside the end boards. On the heavy, chamfered bottom molding extends across the legs. The top is a single board with thumbnail edge and small cleats, over-hanging half an inch at the front, and secured by cotter-pin hinges at the back. The bottom of the chest portion is held by shallow dadoes in the ends, as is the solid bottom below the drawer. The back consists of three boards nailed on horizontally. Inside the top is the usual till. The most interesting feature of this piece is the nicely executed over-all painted design based on vine stems formed into circular loops with highly stylized bell-like flowers, and birds in colors that are hard to determine.

Over-all the chest measures 37½ by 18 inches and is 32¾ inches high. It is thought to have originated in the Taunton, Massachusetts, area.

BASE MOLDING

66

SINGLE-DRAWER BOX CHEST

This is a plain, pine, box-type chest made without a frame in spite of the two drawers that are really one. When this drawer is removed a storage space beneath it is revealed. The flat section between the two drawer panels is actually a piece of ¾-inch wood added to the 1-inch-thick front of the drawer to bring it level with the panel moldings. The moldings themselves are nailed directly to the drawer to give the recessed effect. Apart from this, the drawer is unusual in two respects: The back is housed into the sides, and the bottom is nailed onto both sides and back.

The wide board above the drawer and the narrow one below it are rabbeted into the sides, and set in flush with the edge that borders the drawer space. The back also is rabbeted in and nailed. The lifting top has cotter-pin hinges whose clinched tails are visible in the photograph.

The 18-inch deep lid has the usual end overhang to accommodate a pair of cleats, the ends rounded to continue the line of the thumbnail molding. The large front panel was evidently an irresistible challenge to the artist whose freehand, eye-catching squiggles are a triumph of improvisation.

Over-all, the chest measures 41 by 18 inches, by 36 inches high.

67

PENNSYLVANIA CHEST

Pennsylvanians of German descent were responsible for a large number of board chests decorated in color, of which this is a particularly felicitous example. Here the decoration takes the form of painted panels on the front upper section and the lid, plus floral patterns between the front panels, on the drawers and the ends. The entire chest body is painted blue; the moldings on the base, lid, and banding above the drawers are red. Other colors are black and brown, the panels having white grounds.

This chest has both front and back let into the sides and nailed, the whole resting on corner blocks and rails attached to the inside of the bracket-footed base. The central molding, which projects even with the lid and base, extends around the ends. The drawers are lipped, with twin dovetails, housed bottom, and slide on runners.

This chest dates from the last decade of the 18th century, and several other chests are known with this unicorn and tulip design. This one, a product of Berks County, is of tulip wood, with a yellow pine lid, base and back. The top is 52½ inches long over-all, 23 inches wide, and the chest stands 28⅝ inches high.

68
DOG-TOOTH CHEST—1670

The principal decorative motif of this paneled oak chest is the square dog-tooth design on the front stiles and legs—four leaves radiating from a raised center. It is this pattern that sets it apart from most other such chests carved in low relief. Otherwise, the panel, rail, and drawer decorations are quite common to the late 17th-century period. The chest actually is much heavier than it looks. The drawer front, for example, is 1⅜-inches thick; the sides 1⅛-inches thick, and all oak, the bottom being let into the front and back. Running on slides, the drawer has no need to show a bottom rail. The legs, which have been pieced out to their original length, are 1½ inches thick and 2⅝ inches wide. The top is made from four oak boards held with thin end cleats, and thumbnail molded, the hinges being of the cotter-pin type. The end stiles and top rails spanning the panels are crudely decorated with a pair of chiselled grooves, whereas the bottom rails are properly stop-chamfered. The front pair of stiles are, in contrast, nicely molded. The rail above the dawer also has a simple molding formed down its center, and a reverse ogee (cyma reversa) molding along its bottom edge. Inside the cleat is the usual till, also of oak.

This piece stands 36 inches high, the top measuring 33½ by 18 inches.

DOG-TOOTH ORNAMENT

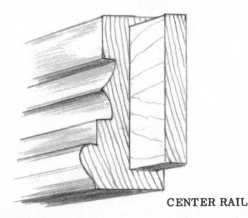

CENTER RAIL

69

OAK CHEST—1693

Here we have a large chest whose single drawer is faced with the tiny panels discussed earlier, the upper part being decorated with split spindles. This chest is made entirely of oak, quarter-sawed, even to the imitation panels and the lid. The latter is held on with a massive pair of cleats, 19¼ inches long and 1 inch wide, which taper from 2 inches thick at the eye to ½ inch at the front end. Each is held to the top by four nails clinched on the upper surface. The back of the chest is paneled, and the uprights are deeply grooved to receive the tenons of both top and back rails and the panel between them. The three front panels are held by moldings formed on the front rails and stiles. The end panels also are let in from the back. The bottom of the chest above the drawer is pinned through the front rail. The name plate, as usual in so many of these pieces, is of smooth pine and let into the oak. All rails are channel molded, and it would seem that this chest would have been sufficiently handsome, with its nice paneling and general proportions, without the help of the spindles—a mere nod to current fashion.

The chest top is 46 inches long, 20 inches deep, and stands 29½ inches high.

TABLE BOX—1690

On top of the chest is a table box made at a time when spindle decoration was in full flower. This box, dated 1690, is a good example of the extremes to which box decoration was sometimes carried. On the front are no less than 25 sunken panels—the sort of work usually reserved for the larger chests. It should be compared with a similar but more restrained example shown in **Fig. 50.** Its dimensions are: 28 by 17¾, by 10 inches high.

Note: In Fig. 49 can be seen the method of constructing the tiny box panels, details of which are described.

70

PANELED OAK CHEST—1690

Unusual in both design and decoration, this oak chest is minus a drawer, only the slides being left to show there ever was one. The lid is of pine, as are the oddly shaped panels. The restored feet are more authentic than they may appear, and there is little doubt that they were originally made separately from the legs, and doweled on. The lid is stiffened with a pair of oak cleats which do not appear to have been too effective in preventing warping. The hinges are the usual iron cotters. Inside the chest is a till of pine whose lid has a molded edge. The oak framing is quite substantial, the front legs being 1⅛ inches thick and 3⅛ inches wide. The back legs are 2 inches thick, with the inside corner beveled off. The thickness of the front legs makes possible stiff tenoned joints with the side rails without those tenons going all the way through the legs. The tenons actually are pinned through the narrow outside edges of the leg. The front bottom-rail tenons are held with a single pin, but the heavier stiles and top rail get two. Each end of the chest is in the form of a thick raised panel with a very wide chamfer to the edges. The legs and stiles are made lighter in appearance by the twin-channel grooving down each front leg and stile, and the single molding of the rails. The pine panels are half the thickness of the stiles and rails, and corner blocks are inserted to bring them flush with the front. These blocks fill in the spaces left by the six- or eight-sided frames that decide the shape of the exposed panels. The weeping-willow pattern in the two outer panels is executed in a brown paint that has suffered because the whole chest had been daubed over with red at one time. Of the central panel's decoration nothing is left but five circular marks on what appears to have been a white background. The dimensions of the chest are: 43 by 19 by 30¾ inches high.

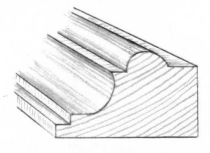

PANEL MOLDING

STILES

71

PANELLED CHEST—1705

The simple, lightweight paneled chest shown here was made in 1705. It is of oak, with a pine lid and back, drawer fronts and panels. The three front panels are held in with loose moldings from the front in the modern manner. The drawer is of the flush type, the sides dovetailed and runs on bottom guides. The chest ends each have two panels, divided at drawer height, and these are set in grooves in the stiles and rails. The bare carcase is decorated with shallow moldings formed down the centers of the rails and legs. The pine top, as usual, overlaps at the ends to accommodate oak cleats, and carries a thumbnail molding on three sides. It is held by cotter-pin hinges clinched into the top surface.

With the 4-inch-wide legs being only a full inch thick, a careful tenoning job had to be done to obtain maximum stiffness and strength, particularly as regards the side rails where the tenons pass right through the stiles and show on the front. The painted decoration of panels and drawer front is prettily done, with an unusual and effective circular date panel worthy of more careful lettering. In addition, the surface is mottled and this does much to hide the side-rail tenons.

The chest is 48¾ inches long, 20½ inches deep, and 33 inches from foot to top.

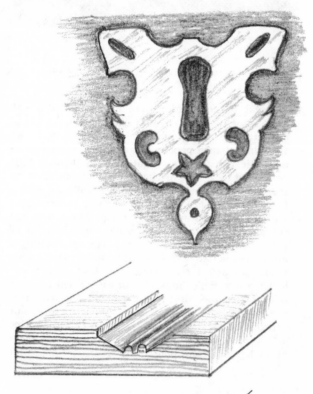

RAILS

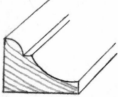

PANEL MOLDING

72

PINE SIX-BOARD CHEST

Something quite different is represented by this simple box chest from America's Southwest, decorated with gouge and scratch carving. Made wholly of sugar pine, the box is held together with random-sized dovetails both back and front. The bottom is nailed on, a form of construction that really calls for iron straps to keep it from falling off when the box is lifted with a load inside. The maker obviously was more artist than craftsman, the poor workmanship being relieved by the deeply carved paterae—a stylized flower design found on many 17th- and 18th-century pieces—which in turn contrast strongly with the scratch carving of prancing dogs (in the East they would be birds!). Both lock and escutcheon are of excellent design, undoubtedly of Spanish origin, the hasp and hinges being quite functional in comparison. The hasp is mildly decorated with its shaped hinge end, curled tail, and notched edges. An interesting survival which could date anywhere from the early 17th century to 1700. The box is 44½ inches long, 17 inches high, and 18½ inches deep.

73

CHEST-ON-FRAME—1775

This ambitious pine piece was made sometime during the last quarter of the 18th century, and it is obviously the work of a country craftsman whose woodworking skill was greater than his ability to design a handsome piece. The sturdy base deserved better underpinnings than the ungainly turned legs; otherwise, the construction is good and the whole is well-proportioned. The deep and bold front and side aprons are tenoned into the upper square section of the 18-inch-long legs. On top of this frame is a heavy molding that serves to seat the chest which rests on the legs. The chest portion is complete in itself, made up of ¾-inch end boards, 18¼ inches wide. Into these are dovetailed the drawer dividers, the top and bottom boards being nailed in. The drawer slides are dadoed into the end boards. The edges of the top are covered by a built-up crown molding. The drawers are lipped slightly, and have multiple dovetails. The brasses are handmade, or at least hand-decorated. One of the handles is upside down. Keyhole escutcheons have been applied to the four large drawers even though none of them has a lock—a common practice on much country furniture as the simplest means of decoration. This piece is 57 inches high. The chest body is 36¼ inches wide (39½ inches over the molding) and 18¼ inches deep (20 inches over molding). The frame is 16 inches high, 39 inches wide, and 19½ inches deep.

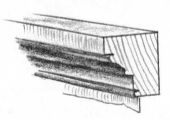

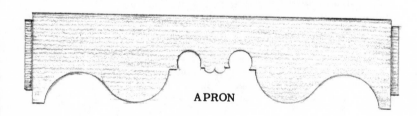

APRON

ESCUTCHEON

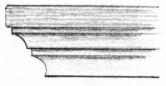

CROWN MOLDING

74

CHEST-ON-FRAME—1690

A combination of pine and oak, this early chest-on-frame is notable for the spool turnings of the front stretcher and legs, a not entirely successful venture judging by the damage the thin turnings have suffered. Even in oak the fine edges are fragile. Another feature is the manner in which the three strips of molding have been carried right across the front, making it appear that the stiles are separate from the legs. In spite of the four knobs and four panels this piece has only one drawer and that is made to look like two. All four panels have unusually wide moldings, the two sections set off by large cove moldings above and below them. The drawer-front molding somewhat belies the rather crude construction of the drawer itself, which has both front and back nailed on, the bottom being housed into back and front. It runs on slides and is all of oak. Eight split spindles on the stiles help to harmonize the turned base with otherwise flat surfaces above it. The ends of the chest above drawer level are enclosed by flat, recessed panels 5½ inches high, with a simple molding on the lower edge of the top rail. The lid is the usual single board with cleats nailed under the ends. Note that the front legs are turned below the stretcher.

The dimensions of this attractive but rather odd specimen are: Length 29¾ inches; width 16½ inches, and height 35¾ inches. The drawer is 3¾ inches deep. The center line of the front stretcher is 5 inches above the floor, and the back and side stretchers are 1 inch thick, 2 inches wide.

DRAWERS

RAIL

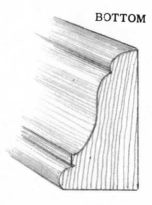

BOTTOM

75

CHEST OF DRAWERS—1690

Properly carried out, the decoration of chests by geometrical moldings can be exceedingly effective, as this example shows. Here the color contrast between the oak chest of drawers and the walnut decoration emphasizes the three-dimensional effect. Another feature of this piece is the air of solidity supplied by the heavy cornice and base moldings, together with the wide, flat corner posts and central stile. This effect is carried out by the deep, square end panels in their heavy, plain framing, separated by a bold molding—the same molding that separates the drawers. On this piece even the front bun feet look perfectly at home. The central molding is carried around the ends as if to indicate that the chest was made in two sections, as many of them were. The sides of the four drawers have a single dovetail at the front, with the back nailed on.

The chest measures 39 by 23½ inches, and is 34¾ inches tall.

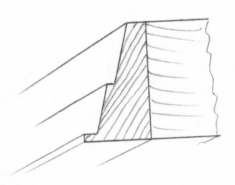

STEP MOLDING

76

TULIP CHEST OF DRAWERS—1690

One of the most skillfully decorated chests, dating from the very late 17th century is this five-drawer example from Connecticut. In order to make the most of the painted designs, whitewood was used for the drawer fronts and pine for the raised end panels. The frame is of oak with a whitewood top. The drawers have oak sides, pine backs and bottoms, and they run on slides. Each end panel displays a beautifully executed large-scale tulip in red and white, framed by a freehand scroll border. That border is repeated, on a smaller scale, around the drawer edges. Even the front corner posts carry a trailing-vine pattern simply to fill the space.

On the drawer fronts are found a variety of motifs found elsewhere—thistles, crowns, fleurs-de-lis, etc. The only repellent note is the pair of human faces from whose mouths the vines on the top drawers issue.

Structurally, the chest is sound except for a warped top, and much-worn slides that now permit the top drawers to sag. The back of the chest is closed with a huge, and quite thick, horizontal panel composed of two boards rabbet-jointed. Single-arch moldings,

⅞ inch wide and ½ inch thick separate the drawers, extending across the front posts. Other moldings lie under the thumbnail-edged top and trim off the base, diverting the eye from the nondescript feet that are merely extensions of the corner posts. The teardrop handles, held by cotter pins through delicate escutcheons, are of the proper period. The drawers are of the earliest type with single dovetails front and back. The bottom is dadoed into the sides and front. Over-all, the chest of drawers measures 44½ inches by 20½ over the top, and is 42⅝ inches high.

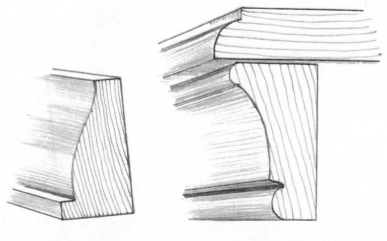

BASE MOLDING   LID & CROWN MOLDING

77

PAINTED CHEST OF DRAWERS

Although built some time after 1850, this Pennsylvania chest of drawers is decorated in the earlier country style. The tiny, formalized tulips, complete with heart-shaped bulbs, are somewhat skimpy and have little relation to the dot-and-stripe borders of drawer edges and corner posts. On the frieze, however, this treatment, combined with the painted reeding, is quite effective giving the appearance of inlay.

The chest is frame-built, with recessed end panels which are decorated with a circular six-petal flower ornament, and bordered with the stenciled dots used elsewhere. Constructed mainly of pine, the chest has drawer fronts of poplar which gives a smoother finish under paint. The dished wooden drawer knobs, also painted, are graduated in size according to the depths of the drawers. The rear feet are extensions of the flat, rectangular corner posts which are considerably wider than the front ones. The latter are square in section, with turned feet that seem small in proportion to the massive chest front that they support.

This chest of drawers is 45¾ wide, 21¾ inches deep, and 45¾ inches tall.

CROWN MOLDING

DRAWER KNOBS

78

OAK AND PINE CHEST OF DRAWERS—1680

Of oak, with a pine top and drawer parts, this small chest has three drawers, each with two panels and a separating dummy stile on the front. The stiles and the molding are applied to the drawer front, the nail heads being left visible. When the drawers are closed the molding is flush with the end stiles and the rails. The rails above and below the center drawer are covered by molding strips across the entire front, giving the effect of three-section piece.

Between the uppermost drawer and the chest top, a cornice effect has been secured with another molding saw-cut vertically into rectangular blocks. The downward extension of the corner stiles to form uncompromisingly plain legs carries ·out the geo-metrical effect of the whole design, extra visual weight being given to the bottom front rail by a wide, projecting molding.

The ends of the piece have twin, flat, sunken panels behind grooved stiles and rails, the latter stop-chamfered top and bottom. Over-all, this distin-guished-looking chest of drawers measures 30 inches wide, 20¼ inches deep, and stands 35½ inches tall. The drawers are 6¾ by 24⅝ inches, the front stiles and legs 2⅝ by 1¾ inches, the panel stiles and rails being 3½ inches and 4 inches wide, respectively. The drawers run on slides, and their bottoms are nailed on.

TOP RAIL

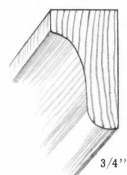

CENTER RAILS

3/4'' X 1 3/8''

79
SHAKER TALL CHEST

Though of early 19th-century vintage, this Shaker chest of drawers is worthy of inclusion because of its utter simplicity which endows it with a certain dignity. The workmanship is perfect. Designed to economize floor space, it enabled everything not actually in use to be neatly stored out of sight. This is a floor-to-ceiling piece that called for steps to reach the upper drawers, the top ones being arranged in pairs to minimize the effort required to open them. The wood for the pine drawer fronts was evidently very carefully chosen, free from knots and blemishes, and painstakingly smoothed before being tinted with a varnish containing a little stain.

The case portion of this piece is extremely simple in construction, the ends being single boards 18 inches wide and 7 feet long. Side cutouts formed feet, raising the drawers four inches from the floor. The apparently small bracket feet are reinforced in the angle with downward tapering blocks. Both top and base are entirely unadorned except for a simple nose molding. All drawers have fronts ¾ inch thick, and lipped ¼ inch. The flat knobs are of maple. The all-pine drawer sides are attached with lap dovetails, the pins small, and the tails large, while the bottoms fit into grooves in front and back. The drawers are separated by rails housed into the end boards, the guides also being held by rabbets and nails, with a cross piece at the back to support the closed drawer. A dust board is let into the supporting members at the bottom. Dimensions: 7 feet tall, 42 inches wide, 18 inches deep. There are six 10-inch and four 8-inch drawers.

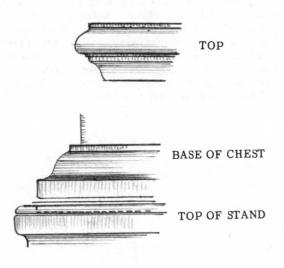

TOP

BASE OF CHEST

TOP OF STAND

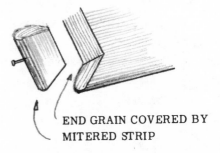

END GRAIN COVERED BY
MITERED STRIP

80

QUEEN ANNE HIGHBOY

A typical country-made pine piece with Queen Anne leanings is this sturdy 5-legged highboy which is painted black and decorated all over—even on the legs and stretcher—with flowers, birds, and bridges, in the Chinese manner. It dates from the early 1700 s, and actually is a common design, far from unique, and simple to copy. Having one long drawer in the base it is obviously a very early type with the strongest form of stretcher arrangement. The base construction is quite simple, with the legs doweled through the bottom board as well as the stretcher. The front edge of the board is rounded off, and mitered back at the ends to receive a nosing strip that covers the end grain. At each corner is a vertical block into which a leg dowel passes upward. This block is mortised to receive the tenons of the end boards and the back board. The pegs can be seen in the photograph. Around the top of this section a heavy molding is applied. This molding extends a ¼ inch above the body of the base, forming a recess into which the upper drawer section can be housed. This upper unit has a wide base molding formed on the front and ends of its bottom board. The lower ends of the sides are housed in blind dadoes in the top of this board and pegged or nailed from below. A blind-rabbeted top board with three molded edges is applied in the same manner. The end boards are rabbeted to receive the drawer dividers, and all exposed edges are covered with half-round molding, notched, and nailed. All drawers are flush-fronted, the sides having twin dovetails, both the sides and front being dadoed to receive the bottom. The teardrop handles appear to be original, but whether there were ever any lock escutcheons, or what became of them it is impossible to determine. The over-all dimensions of this piece are: Height 52 inches, width 39½ inches, depth 15 inches.

81

MAPLE HIGHBOY—1775

The craftsman who built this maple highboy had a good eye for proportion, but fell down when he came to do the cabriole legs. Also he made things difficult for himself when he made four of them instead of only the front pair so that the piece is forced to stand out several inches from the wall. Rear legs are quite often made straight for this reason. Incidentally, these legs have square sections extending upward to form corner posts of the base. A problem was also introduced when the long drawer was built into the base over three other drawers. The horizontal dividing strip (the rail) is dovetailed into the front legs. The apron beneath the three drawers had to be cut out to receive them, leaving only two narrow vertical strips to be notched into this rail. And pins had to be inserted through these strips to hold the center drawer guides. Pins of a darker wood were used for all tenons, and for attaching the base and crown moldings, with no attempt to hide them. All drawers are lipped, and the five top ones are nicely graded as to depth. Since the uppermost of these is a single drawer (instead of a pair as is more usual) substantial steps must have been needed in opening it. All drawers have their full quota of dovetails as might be expected at the date given—another indication of painstaking workmanship. The dimensions are: Height 72 inches, depth of top over molding 19½ inches, side 17½ inches, width of top over molding 39¾ inches, front 36 inches. The base is 19½ inches deep and 39 inches wide.

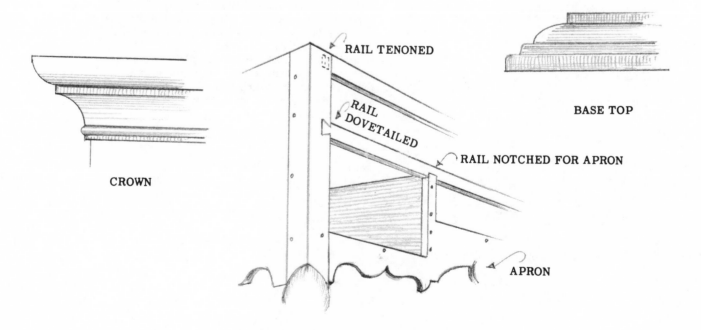

CROWN

RAIL TENONED

RAIL DOVETAILED

RAIL NOTCHED FOR APRON

BASE TOP

APRON

SECTION V

Cupboards and Dressers,
Dry Sink, Wardrobe

Old-time cupboards appear in many guises, from the original cupboards consisting of an open shelf or side board on which cups and related objects were stood or displayed, to the hutch which in the beginning was a cupboard with a door, and the livery cupboard which had no door. At that time there was also the double-decked court cupboard, also doorless, that later acquired an enclosed section on the upper shelf (called an ambry and originally a receptacle for arms), and the press cupboard that had enclosed spaces on both shelves and still does, though there are a great many varieties, some with drawers below instead of cupboards (using that word in its modern sense!) Press cupboards likewise can have the splayed cupboard on the upper deck in the manner of the court cupboard. All of these hutches, court and press cupboards were made and used by colonists in the early 17th century, the exception being the livery cupboard of which but few examples are known and these quite likely of English origin. The hutch cupboard, which was very similar in construction, with ventilated fronts and small doors, is more readily identifiable as of American make.

In the 18th century most of these pieces gave way to a wide variety of cupboards—wall or hanging types, corner cupboards open and closed, glazed or paneled; cupboards on high legs, cupboards on cupboards, and cupboards on chests. In the dining room the court cupboard was replaced by a dresser—open shelves over a cupboard base, often incorporating drawers. In the bedroom there was the wardrobe, with or without drawers and shelves, some few Dutch clothes cupboards of the massive type called *kas,* these lasting in popularity until people began building clothes closets in their bedrooms.

From the cupboard we turn to the dresser, to be replaced in the later, more formal homes with the sideboard which for the most part was beyond the skill of the country joiner even had there been a demand for such a status symbol in the farm house and smaller country home.

82

HUTCH CUPBOARD—1650-1670

A wholly delightful piece of country furniture-making is this late 17th-century hutch which is as beautifully styled at the ends as in front. Made entirely of oak, it has two open panels at the front and two in each end. These are in grille form, made of square-section sticks set in at a 45-degree angle to the front. The top and bottom rails, and the central one that separates the ventilated cupboard from the closed one beneath it, are carved with the familiar arch pattern. Smaller arches adorn the stiles on either side the small doors. Below each grille is a panel held in with well-defined mitered moldings, and decorated in the center with heavy bosses formed of large molding sections mitered to form squares. Both upper and lower doors, hung on dovetail hinges, have the same panel molding, with slightly smaller bosses tilted 45 degrees to stand on one corner. The lower end panels are flat and sunken, the three rails and the central stiles being grooved longitudinally.

The sturdy frame is strongly tenoned and pinned, and the top is formed of a single board finished with a thumbnail molding on three sides and pinned into the posts. The upper door is held closed with iron staples and two links of chain. As the picture reveals, about 4 inches of leg have been added to restore them to their normal length. This brings the total height to 31 inches. The hutch top is 47 inches long and 22 inches deep.

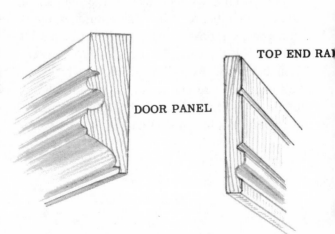

DOOR PANEL

TOP END RA[IL]

PANEL BLOCKS

83

VIRGINIA COURT CUPBOARD

There is nothing crude or unfinished about this court cupboard from Virginia, which is to be expected since most of the Southern furniture was intended for the better homes. The fact that the top is of pine, and fastened with the original pins, and that the cupboard interiors are also of pine, indicates that this is a Colonial piece in spite of the large bulb turnings so characteristic of English work of the Elizabethan and Jacobean periods persisting in America well after the middle of the 17th century. The drawer—one in spite of seeming to be two—

and one door are restorations, as is the shelf and the blocks with the tulip carvings. An interesting feature is the carved bottom rail which continues across the ends. The door panels also are duplicated on the sides. The drawer, having no rail beneath it, is carried on guides.

This product of an unknown cabinetmaker of 1640-1660 measures 48½ inches in length, 19 inches in depth, and at present stands 48 inches tall, the feet being well worn.

84

COURT CUPBOARD—1640-1660

Considerable effort was expended to make this cupboard as ornate as possible with carving, turnings, moldings, applied decorations, and a fancy drop, so that the varicolored inlays seem not only superfluous but out of keeping. This piece is of oak with pine shelves, the upper and lower turnings being made separately and doweled to the blocks. Attention is called to this by the fact that the shelves were bored through so that the uprights could be assembled after the tops were in place. The lower front legs are replacements, as are the feet and the blocks above them. The triangular decorative strips on the front and sides are of pine, colored, and applied to the surface with tiny wooden pins.

The upper posts clear the cupboard stiles by about half an inch. These stiles are inlaid in the same manner as the doors and the rail immediately above the drawers. The inlay is formed of alternating dark and light strips of wood let into the surfaces to a ⅜-inch depth. The heavy, paneled oak doors are hinged on dowels let into the frame about 1½ inches from the end stiles. It should be noted that the carved drawer and rail decorations are carried around the ends of the piece above and below the sunken panels, and under the lower platform. The drawers obviously run on slides, and the manner in which their mitered molding is attached is betrayed by the exposed nailheads. The dimensions of this piece (supposedly unique in design) are: 55½ inches high, 52 inches long, and 23 inches deep.

85

PINE PRESS CUPBOARD—1700

yond the edges of the side members below the drawer helps to conceal the fact that these members are merely plain boards, with no brackets to give them a look of solidity. The surface, unfortunately, has some cloudy finish that gives the pine a look of characterless whitewood, yet this is altogether a "different" piece whose simplicity is its greatest source of charm. Its dimensions are: Height 48½ inches, length 37¼, depth 18 inches.

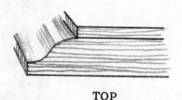

TOP

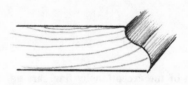

BOTTOM

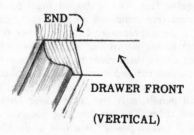

END

DRAWER FRONT

(VERTICAL)

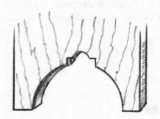

FOOT

One of the plainest in design but neatest in appearance of any antique press cupboard is this pine piece made by some capable craftsman with an artist's eye over 250 years ago. The ends are single boards cut out at one end to form feet, the outer edges of the front boards molded to form a bead in the angle; the overhanging top with an ogee lip worked into three edges, the shelf with a thumbnail edge, an ogee molding below and above a drawer, formed on the front edge of each horizontal board dadoed into the ends. At each end of the drawer is still another strip carefully applied. The four horizontal molded edges emphasize the proportions of each section and add a decorative note that culminates in the pair of turned posts between shelf and top. The upper and lower doors set in the center add a pair of vertical lines that break up the flat front, while their heavy, raised panels add an emphatic note that gives the piece character. The doors are mounted on hairpin hinges, and they, and the drawer, have small but shapely turned knobs. The upper door is set between the two oblique sides without benefit of stiles against which to close, suggesting, along with other features, that the purpose was to create a piece of furniture with the minimum of parts. The fact that the whole front projects be-

86

PRESS CUPBOARD—1690-1700

In spite of the exceptionally fine carving, this press-type cupboard is of simple design and construction, bearing the earmarks of the country cabinetmaker. All four legs are of the same dimensions with plain, rectangular feet. The scalloped brackets and lower rail decoration, confined to the front, do little to improve the appearance. The two lower drawers are shown without hardware, and the decorative torus molding above them hides the third drawer's vertical joints behind the end carvings. The cupboard in the upper section has the usual splayed ends, with plain recessed panels, only the center door having carved rails and stiles. The overhanging cornice, supported by heavy, turned posts, has a row of dentils over the carved frieze. The frieze itself is interrupted by three chamfered blocks, a common device on these pieces. The blocks are repeated over the sides of the posts.

This piece being of the 1600-1700 period, it is no surprise to find added decoration in the form of split spindles—one pair of them on each side of the cupboard door—and split bosses on the square tops of the posts. The end panels are flat and recessed behind molded rails, and cut into the legs. At the front, this rail is saw-cut to represent two rows of oblong blocks with broken joints. The back of the upper section is a ¾-inch board which the side panel of the cupboard strikes at a 45-degree angle. This joint is concealed by a flat strip about an inch wide nailed over it—a rather ugly device. The strip rests on top of the apron molding that follows the line of the cupboard front from one end of the top to the other.

The principal dimensions of this press cupboard are: Height 58 inches, width 49¾ inches, depth 22¾ inches.

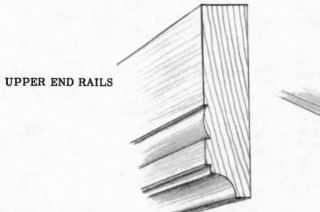

UPPER END RAILS

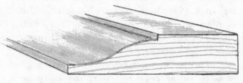

CUPBOARD TRIM

87

PENNSYLVANIA DRESSER

Here is a triumph of the Pennsylvania German craftsman's art—a walnut dresser dating from the early 18th century and probably unique in design— a piece of domestic architecture in wood! This is a piece of furniture lacking in subtlety but splendid in its forthright design and massive construction, the only delicate touches being the ornamental brasses, the rattail hinges, and the finely wrought door catches. The dresser is made in two sections, the lower half having a stack of five equal-sized lipped drawers, flanked by cupboards with heavily framed doors each enclosing two square, raised panels. The panels, it should be noted, have their bevels slightly hollowed. All stiles and rails are unusually wide, and fastened with many nails to the edges of the end, base, and counter boards. The back, likewise, is nailed on so that the ends are totally enclosed. The end grain of the counter is covered by a simple molding. A wider molding at right angles to this extends inward over the top a couple of inches to seat against the side member of the upper shelved section. This lower cabinet rests on three sets of feet, 3 inches high, extending from front to back.

On either side of the drawers is a vertical, transverse partition held by nails through the stiles, and supporting a single shelf dadoed into both end and partition. The upper section, holding two shelves, has molded stiles surmounted by a heavy, built-up dentiled cornice. The shallow upper shelf is dadoed in and edged with a strip of band molding that extends the full length of the interior and behind the stiles. Below it is the other shelf, with a strip of wide molding on its front edge. This strip carries on its face a length of nosing, spaced away from it sufficiently to form long slots that serve as a spoon rack. This shelf is mortised into each end of the cabinet with four separate tenons. Below this shelf is a pair of small, quarter-round (quadrant) shelves that fill in the corners behind the wide stiles. Vertical tongue-and-groove boards nailed to the shelves form the closed back.

Over-all dimensions are: Height 83¾ inches, width 75½ inches, depth 23½ inches.

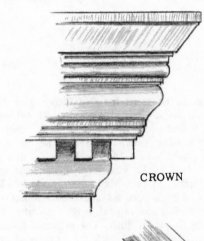

CROWN

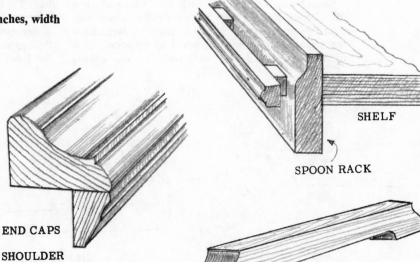

SHELF

SPOON RACK

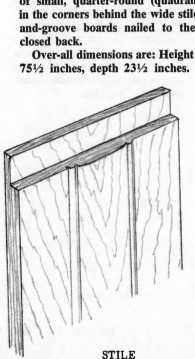

END CAPS

SHOULDER

STILE

FOOT

88

CUPBOARD—1700

Monumental is the word for this heavy pine cupboard, thanks to the heavy moldings. It evidently was ceiling height and probably built in, but there is now no trace of a crown molding. The sides are made from single boards 26½ inches wide, and cut back at a height of 32 inches from the floor to a mere 14½ inches to form the upper cupboard. The front edges of both sections are rabbeted back so that the front stiles and top rail, with their attendant molding, can be set in flush. The setback, forming a 12-inch counter, is faced with the horizontal strip of mitered molding that surrounds the lower cupboard door. Two wide strips of fluted molding flank the upper door, giving the effect of pilasters. And, of course, a great deal of work went into the making of the two doors with their quadruple triangular panels. The sketch shows how they are constructed, and the profiles of the moldings. An interesting feature of the upper door is the difference between the width of the top rail and the bottom one. But both cupboards are rigid in construction, neither becoming out of square in 250 years. An ingenious item is the installation of two drawers below the upper door, the lower edges of their fronts almost touching the counter top. This, of course, necessitated a raised floor for the upper cupboard. The back of the piece is composed of vertical planks nailed on. The major dimensions are: Height 75 inches—43 inches for the top section, 32 inches for the lower one. Across the front this unit measures 39 inches.

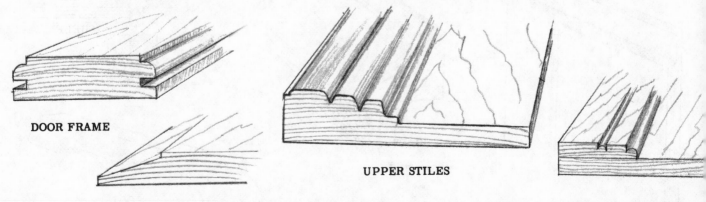

DOOR FRAME

UPPER STILES

LOWER STILE & RAIL

PANEL

89

PINE DRESSER—1800

A well-known style of kitchen dresser is this New England pine piece with scalloped sides matching its frieze, and three plain doors below. This particular dresser has, for reasons of height, lost its cornice molding and top, which probably was something like that shown in the sketch. Having been more or less "built in," as the wainscot notch in the back edge of the end board reveals, the ends are made in one piece and there is no back. Quite often the movable dressers were made with the shelf section detachable, and the back was closed by vertical lap-jointed boards.

In this unit the shelves are made of thick pine boards, housed in the ends which are nailed through. The top is likewise housed where it abuts the end boards, the rest of it overlapping the cut-away portions as well as the front stiles. As this piece is entirely of board construction, the top, or counter, is supported at the front edge by four strips of board, two being the narrow end stiles, and two—one wide and one narrow—separating the three doors. The base consists of a 2-inch rail fastened to the end boards and the stiles. Since there is no back, the counter top needs to be supported at the rear in a similar manner.

The doors are made from single boards ⅞ inch thick, hung on cast-iron butt hinges that date from this period. Clothespin knobs and wooden catches are used, the doors closing against the shelf edges. For rigid construction there should be a top rail at the front with the stiles tenoned into it. However, except for the well-shaped scallops, this is apparently a homemade job that has done well to survive 160 years. Dimensions are: Length 63 inches, depth 16¼ inches, base 31 inches high; shelf base 9¼ inches deep; shelves 6½ inches back to front. The first shelf is 14 inches up from the counter, the second shelf spaced 10½ inches above the first, the third one 8½ inches, and the top 15 inches to allow for the hanging scalloped border which is 5 inches high. The total height of the piece (without the missing cornice and top board) is therefore 81 inches from the floor.

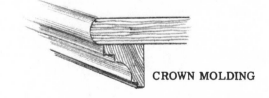

CROWN MOLDING

90

SMALL PINE DRESSER—1720-1750

A mellow all-pine dresser that is perfect for the display of antique pewter is shown here. The base is a plain board cupboard but the upper shelf section is a work of art. The opening is framed with a well-designed and perfectly executed series of sweeping cyma curves. A neat cornice emphasizes the rigid squareness of the two sections below it, while the thick base molding and the wide stiles add a touch of weight where it is needed.

The sides of this dresser are made of single boards, 14½ inches wide up to counter level, and 7¾ inches wide above it. Two ¾-inch boards, 73 inches long and 17½ inches wide, form the back. The three boards forming the top opening are nailed to the sides, the vertical members resting on the counter. In the base section there is no rail above the door, but there is one at the bottom just wide enough to clear the 3½-inch base molding. The 18¾-inch-wide door is made up of one wide and one narrow boards with a pair of end cleats, breadboard fashion. It is hung on iron H hinges and held closed with a wooden turnbutton. At one time there was a lock of which only the keyhole escutcheon now remains. Inside the cupboard is one shelf.

Principal dimensions are: Height 73 inches, width 35¼ inches, depth: lower section 16 inches, upper section 9¼ inches. Height of top section is 38 inches, Top rail is 8¾ inches deep, counter width 38 inches. Base molding 1⅛ by 3½ inches. The sides, lower front, and back are ¾ inch thick, the upper facings ⅝ inch thick. The door is 18¾ inches by 30⅝.

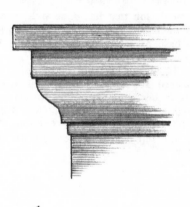

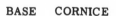

BASE   CORNICE

91

LARGE PINE DRESSER—1730-1770

As unusually large kitchen dresser, this make a fine display of scrubbed white pine. The design, though not particularly attractive, is inoffensive. The counter is almost three feet high, and the shelf section more than four feet higher so that the topmost shelf is more for display than utility. The cornice molding is thick enough to give a nice balance without appearing topheavy.

Made throughout of 1-inch-thick pine, the dresser has a backless base and a separate shelf unit with uninspired scrollwork. The three drawers are slightly lipped, their sides being held with twin dovetails at front and back, with the thick bottom chamfered to fit into grooves in the front and sides, the back edge being nailed. The drawers run on guides, and they have small wooden knobs which seem quite inadequate.

The end cupboards are floored at sill height, and have one-shelf housed into the ends and partitions. The nicely paneled doors are hung on 4-inch H hinges, with tiny knobs and thumb catches. In the top section the shelves are dadoed into the ends and supported elsewhere by nails through the back. This back consists of wide, horizontal boards.

Over the right-hand cupboard is a slide 19 inches wide that pulls out to 14 inches from the base top rail. It has a front lip to fill the opening neatly, and a rear one to prevent its being accidentally pulled all the way out. A wide, flat grip attached to the front edge serves as a handle.

The major dimensions of this piece are: Height 86 inches, length 72½ inches, base depth 17¾ inches, height 35½ inches. Shelf section is 7 inches deep (shelves 6 inches); the drawers are 31½ inches long, with fronts 7¾, 8½, and 9½ inches deep respectively. The cupboard doors are 15 inches wide.

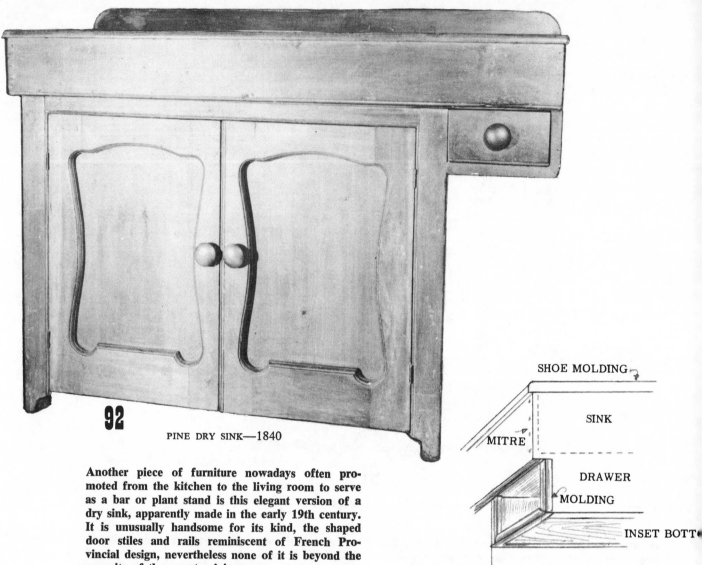

92

PINE DRY SINK—1840

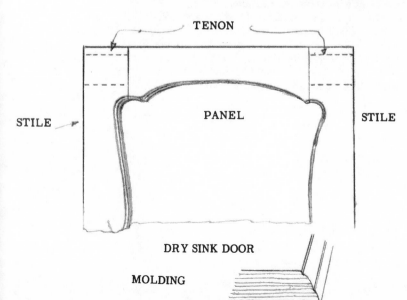

SHOE MOLDING

SINK

MITRE

DRAWER

MOLDING

INSET BOTT

TENON

STILE · PANEL · STILE

DRY SINK DOOR

MOLDING

Another piece of furniture nowadays often promoted from the kitchen to the living room to serve as a bar or plant stand is this elegant version of a dry sink, apparently made in the early 19th century. It is unusually handsome for its kind, the shaped door stiles and rails reminiscent of French Provincial design, nevertheless none of it is beyond the capacity of the country joiner.

The top, which is of ⅞-inch material, is 48 inches by 20 inches over-all, and stands 34 inches high. Finishing the top edge of the ⅞-inch-thick sides is a ⅞ by 1¼-inch shoe molding. Across the front is a ⅞-inch-thick, 4⅞-inches-deep apron which provides a ⅞-inch overhang at the left end. At the right-hand end is a 12-inch overhang beyond the cabinet base. This is made 10¼ inches deep below

the sink lip to accommodate a drawer. The drawer sides are nailed to the rabbeted front and squared back, and the bottom is inset flush. This slides on the bottom board of the overhanging section which is nailed to the end board and to the cabinet side. The front edges of the end board and the bottom are covered by ½-inch-thick mitered trim. Across the back of the 5-inch-deep sink is a ¾-inch board 8 inches deep.

In the cabinet section, two stiles which form the legs, and a narrow top rail enclose a pair of doors 16⅝ inches wide and 24¼ inches high. The molding is quite simple and the door frames are assembled in the usual manner with substantial tenons. The boards forming the panels actually are square and of ¼-inch pine nailed to the backs of the frames. Inside the cabinet are two shelves, ¾-inch thick, housed at the ends and nailed to the back, as is the cabinet bottom, against the front edge of which the doors close, 2½ inches from the floor.

93

SHAKER CUPBOARD-ON-CHEST—1820-30

Of nicely grained pine, the cupboard-on-chest is built as a unit, the vertical cupboard dividers being let into the chest top, and the end boards extending in one piece from the base to the full height. The top of this piece is a flat board, flush at the ends and projecting in front only to the face of the doors. The two doors are hinged to four-inch stiles and meet against the end of an internal partition. The purpose of this partition is to make the cupboard usable by two persons, giving each equal privacy. The flat panels are set into the doors from the inside where they are held by quarter-round molding. A similar, narrow molding is formed on the outside of the stiles and rails. All of the door rails are extra-wide—five to eight inches—so that they are never likely to warp or bend.

In the chest section the rails separating the drawers are attached to the sides by shouldered, housed joints that do not show from the front. The drawers are lipped, and slide on runners. Their sides are lap-dovetailed front and rear, the bottom fitting into grooves in the front and back boards. These drawers are all pine. The runners are rabbeted into the ends of the frame and nailed, while supporting rails are carried across the back. The base of this chest is finished with a plain, mitered strip which is not even chamfered.

Dimensions are: Chest 42¾ inches wide, 33 inches high, 15⅝ inches deep. Cupboard: 40¾ inches wide, 47 inches high, 11½ inches deep. Overall height is 6 feet 8 inches.

94

SHAKER WARDROBE—1850

However hard the Shaker craftsmen tried to eliminate the decorative from their furniture designs they were not always able to resist adding a gay touch to an otherwise strictly utilitarian piece. This tall cherry wardrobe, made in Kentucky in the mid-19th century, is a good example, its uncompromising four-square rigidity betrayed by the sweeping curves of its base. On the other hand, the doors could not be plainer; at the front there is not even a stopped chamfer to set off the panels. The panels are set in from the rear where they are held by small quarter-round molding. The doors close against the sides of the board that divides the interior into two sections and, incidentally, stiffens the whole structure. Each section has its own lock so that the wardrobe can be used by two persons in complete privacy.

The door stiles and rails are fastened from the inside so that the pins do not show on the front, a feature not found in most pieces. The mitered 45-degree crown rising above the top board is held by glue blocks. The wardrobe sides are of single boards from floor to crown molding. These are cut out at the bottom to form bracket feet 9 inches high. Inset vertical boards enclose the back.

At one side of the central partition there is a shelf 11¾ inches from the top, with a hanging bar below it, and six metal clothes hangers. On the other side there is a similar shelf, with two other shelves below it 16¾ inches apart. This piece is 83 inches high, 49 inches wide, and 18⅝ inches deep. Each of the two doors is 65⅞ inches by 23⅞ inches. It is interesting to compare this piece with similar cupboards made sixty years earlier as to structural details.

95

CORNER CUPBOARD—18TH CENTURY

Of the Connecticut Valley type, this built-in style of corner cupboard has strong architectural features; the pillars, arch and keystone, and the beautifully shaped lower doors with their molded raised panels in particular. The design of the glazed doors, with their varying sizes and shapes of panes adds a delicate note of refinement and dignity. Inside, the cupboard has a molded shell top, built up from individual strips (though some are cut out of the solid). This rests on a molded cornice which terminates at the front in a pair of fluted pilasters. The three shelves follow the curve of the rounded back and have the usual circular central projection. Lining these shelves up with the glazing bars is responsible for the bottom glass panes being shorter than the rest.

The whole structure is carefully built up of small-dimensioned lumber. Each of the fluted pilasters flanking the doors is composed of two boards joined at 135 degrees. The pillow block above is formed in one piece with the fillet and cove molding on one edge and a simple bead on the other. The "keystone" likewise is made in one piece with its moldings, but the spandrels, filling the spaces between pilasters and arch, are built up with a mitered frame and panel. The arch itself is in two sections, with a tiny quarter-round molding on the inside. This rests on another strip jointed higher up on the curve and finished on its inner edge with a nosing fillet following the bend of the curve.

Each curved section of the upper door frame is composed of two sections doweled together and tenoned only to the meeting stile. The two lower doors are of normal construction, with twin panels. All doors are mounted on large HL hinges that serve to stiffen the right-angle joints. The upper hinges of the round-topped doors are of the simple H style, their tops reaching the springing point of the arches. Note the delicate glazing bars (sticking) which, thanks to the rigidity of the door frames and their careful fitting, have withstood almost 200 years of use. The major dimensions of this piece are: Height 8 feet 5½ inches, width 6 feet 2½ inches.

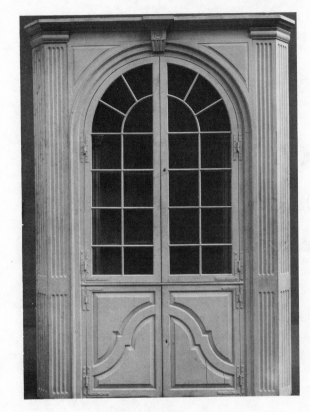

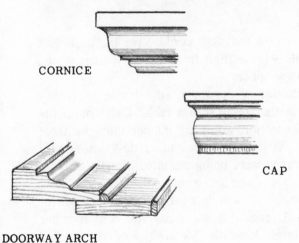

CORNICE

CAP

DOORWAY ARCH

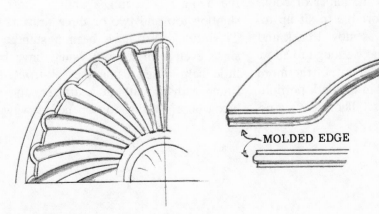

SHELL DETAIL

MOLDED EDGE

SHELF

SECTION VI

Desk-On-Frame, Desk With Drawers,
Slant-Top Desk, Secretary

All of these are allied pieces of furniture, many of which were made by country craftsmen from early Colonial days. The first table-top desks were merely boxes with a slanting top for writing or, perhaps oftener, for reading. Since these desk boxes had to be lifted, their size and weight was necessarily limited. Putting the desk on its own stand turned it into a respectable piece of furniture instead of an accessory. Now it could be made in a really useful size and with ample internal compartments. But, for writing or reading, the top had to be closed, and perhaps fitted with a ledge—a strip of molding to hold the paper or book. Even so, it was not comfortable to sit up to, unless the base stretcher was moved back and the frame apron made shallow enough to allow room for the knees. Many did not; furthermore there was usually a drawer in the desk portion, and perhaps one in the base. Those having no

drawer in the desk could have the desk box made with a high front so as to increase its storage space.

Putting a drawer in the frame in reality made the frame into a table. Quite often the desk portion was then smaller than the table top. At the same time other desk boxes with a drawer were being mounted directly on legs, the tops of the legs forming the stiles. As likely as not, the desk box would then be made of boards enclosing the stiles and held together by large dovetails. Meanwhile other so-called desks of a primitive type were being made in the manner of a tall, six-board chest with a slanting top and two or three drawers below. This, too, must have been a standing desk since even a high stool would have been of little help. Then came the fall-front desk, a frame with or without a drawer, and a desk box whose slanting top opened downward instead of upward, and came to rest on a pair of slides built into the desk bottom. The early slides were square in section and quite heavy. Later, it was found that thinner ones, several inches deep and set on edge, did a better job.

Since the lowered desk top, or lid, now projected well beyond the front of the desk base, the user was able to sit up to it and write on a horizontal, flat surface. An early alternative was a desk with a lifting top and a narrow drop front, 6 to 8 inches high. Such a desk would need a shallow apron for knee room and no front stretcher to obstruct the user's

legs. Its chief merit was that it provided plenty of storage space between the top, when closed, and the writing surface.

During the 18th century other outward-opening slant-top desks were built with chests of drawers or low cupboards for a base. It was not long thereafter that the wide and shallow top of such a desk was found ideal for use as a base for tall shelves or a cupboard—a combination known to us today as a secretary. Generally, such dual units were made in one piece, but in Connecticut the two-piece secretary seems to have been favored.

96

DESK-ON-FRAME—1800

This is either a clerk's or schoolmaster's desk, and is made of pine throughout except for the pigeonholes. The base is a simple, four-square structure, the four long legs held rigidly by the stretchers and the four deep aprons tenoned into them. Both the aprons and stretchers are flush with the outer faces of the legs. The front apron, which is beaded at the lower edge, is in one piece, with a rectangular opening in its center to receive the drawer. The drawer front is, or was, slightly lipped, the ends rabbeted back to receive the sides which are blind-dovetailed on. The back is nailed on, but the bottom is let into the sides and front in the modern manner. So as to be out of the way when not in use, the drawer handle is of the bail type. The top faces of the apron and the legs are covered with a mitered molding which serves

to hold the desk in position. The desk is a self-contained unit—a simple box with a slat top and drop lid. The front and back boards of this box are dovetailed into the ends. The 4-inch fixed top supports the lid on a pair of butt hinges, which are quite sufficient since the lid is ⅞ inch thick. The lid battens, shown in the "open" photograph, are recent additions. Under the fixed top is a nest of pigeonholes and storage spaces. These are made of maple since the main parts are only ¼ inch thick, and the partitions dadoed into the top shelf are only ⅛ inch thick. The piece stands 50½ inches tall, and is 37½ inches long over the frame. The desk unit is 35¼ inches long. From back to front, the desk measures 24½ inches, and the frame 25½ inches over-all.

97

X-STRETCHER DESK-ON-FRAME—1700

This walnut slant-top desk on legs has quite a few attractive features, some of which are obvious at first sight. The original dovetail hinges, the top's wide, overhanging thumbnail molding, the heavy single-arch molding around the drawer, the finely turned legs, the onion feet, and the sweeping curves of the stretcher with its pointed ends combine naïveté and sophistication in a fascinating manner.

The construction of the case is unusual in having the front board extend down alongside the drawer ends, leaving very little wood between the drawer opening and the dovetails. Below the drawer a 2-inch rail is inserted, ending flush with the bottommost dovetail pins. That this construction is faulty is indicated by the cracks in the front board almost level with the drawer opening. The leg section is made separately, with the blocks doweled to the bottom of the case. The leg turnings, although beautiful, are a little too fine even for walnut, as the broken disks bear witness. The stretchers are cut out of 2¾ by 7/16-inch stock, the lapped junction being invisibly pinned. The drawer is made with a single dovetail at the front. The back member of the drawer is dovetailed at its ends to hold the sides, instead of the sides holding on the back. The bottom is recessed into the front and sides, and the drawer runs on guides.

The narrow, flat portion of the desk top, 6⅛ inch deep, is pegged to the ends, while the back is recessed into the top and ends and also pegged. Inside the desk are the usual pigeonholes. The desk is 38 inches long, with a ¾-inch-thick top. The height at the back is 32½ inches; at the front 29¼, while the slant top is one board 15½ inches wide.

98

PINE DESK—1710

A maple middle stretcher—unexplained—is the only part of this desk that is not made of pine. The applied molding just above the drawer, which is carried around the ends, serves to conceal the junction of the base of the desk and the top of the frame. The desk bottom actually is set into the four sides, the back being rabbeted in. The front and ends are held by heavy dovetails, and the bottom is firmly pinned into the top of the legs. A ⅞-inch thick top rail is tenoned into the 2 by 2-inch legs at the front, and a 1½-inch stone-molded rail is similarly held below the drawer. A 5-inch apron on ends and back is likewise tenoned into the legs. All three have a simple bead along the lower edge.

Square-sectioned 2 by 2-inch stretchers with corner beads top and bottom join the front and back legs 4¾ inches from the floor. A similar middle stretcher (the maple one) ties these two end stretchers together. The drawer is 3¾ inches high over the lips, and its sides are held to the front with blind dovetails in pairs. The drawer bottom is recessed into all four sides, and runs on guides. The knob is a simple peg type.

The top of the desk displays a large pair of butterfly hinges, and is finished with a thumbnail molding. A strip of molding nailed to the lid from a book or paper rest. This has a section cut from its center where a lock hasp was formerly located. Inside, the back of the desk is fitted with thin horizontal and vertical partitions to provide six pigeonholes and two drawers.

This desk stands 38 inches high at the back and 29½ inches high at the front. The top is 29 inches long; the level portion 8¾ inches deep, while the lid measures 17 inches down the slant.

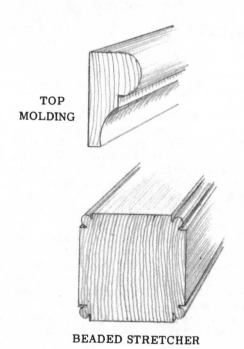

TOP MOLDING

BEADED STRETCHER

99

SLANT-TOP DESK—1700-1710

This slant-top desk, shown in its original condition when acquired, is made of Virginia walnut. Obviously it has suffered considerable damage, yet it is capable of being restored without too many replacements to its pristine state as a handsome piece, relying but little on decoration. Missing is the grooved molding from the drawer separators and the end of the base. The dovetailed front strip holding the lid has come adrift slightly, allowing the lid to fall in at the top. Two butt hinges hold the drop lid which is to be supported by a pair of early-type slides with brass knobs (later slides were thin and deep!). The panel above the top drawers indicates a storage space below the writing surface, with access through a sliding panel. The drawers are flush and of two-front dovetail construction. The desk carcase is held together with dovetails hidden by the molding. The bottom is nailed on and covered by the heavy base mold characteristic of such solidly ball-footed pieces. The flat top section, it will be noted, is set in between the ends. This is probably one of the first of this type of desk with the top swinging down and forward instead of up. Until about 1700 the desk top swung upward, exposing a more or less deep boxlike interior that served for storage and often was equipped with pigeonholes and sometimes small drawers, usually in the upper part so as to be more accessible. Swinging the top down made it possible to use the interior along with the inside of the lid as a writing surface. With the earlier upswinging lid, that lid had to be closed for use as a writing (or reading) surface. Dimensions of this pieces are; Height 40½ inches, width 33¾ inches, depth 20 inches.

BASE

EDGE

INSIDE EDGE OF
ENDS FLUSH

FOOT

100

DESK ON FRAME—1700

Here we have a desk-on-frame in red gumwood, made in New York State around 1700. This piece is of particular interest as foreshadowing the type of desk that was to supersede it—the slant-top, with the top opening downward and outward to serve as a writing surface. This is indicated by the inclusion of a pair of dummy drawers which actually are nothing more than decorative panels. The storage compartment, as will be seen, is quite shallow in front behind the panels); the top slopes at a comfortably flat angle. On the other hand, the presence of a front stretcher renders it difficult to sit up close, and the delicate turnings of that stretcher make it unwise to use it as a footrest. Apart from utility, however, this is a highly decorative piece, in spite of the small, doweled-on turnings hanging from the aprons. The leg turnings are quite individual. As usual, the base is made separately from the desk, with an edge molding extending beyond the frame to match the desk lid overhang. The ends of the top are braced by a pair of cleats which also are similarly molded, and the lower edge carries a light strip of molding to keep papers, etc., from sliding off. The desk is dovetailed together at the four corners, the pegged-on bottom and its front being covered by a small, neat molding. Between the two front "panels" is a nondescript keyhole escutcheon. This unit is 35¼ inches high, 33¾ inches long, and 24 inches front to back.

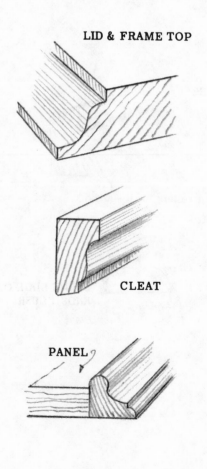

LID & FRAME TOP

CLEAT

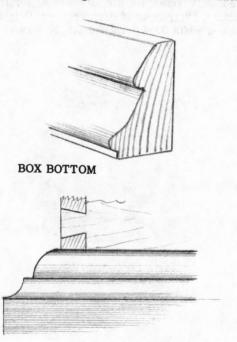

BOX BOTTOM

PANEL

FRAME MOLDING

101

BALL-FOOT SECRETARY—1690

Only the drop lid of this two-piece ball-foot secretary is of pine, the rest being of poplar stained to look like walnut. It dates back to 1690-1700, and has some interesting features, though it does not altogether represent a first-class piece of cabinetwork.

The two parts—a desk forming the base, and a cupboard resting on it—are not exactly mates. The cupboard is actually 1½ inches deeper from front to back than the top of the desk. This made it necessary, a long time ago, to add small, triangular brackets extending backward from the desk sides, level with the top. These give extra support to the cupboard while making the cupboard overhang at the back less noticeable. There seems no doubt that

both pieces were made by the same craftsman, and the desk interior in particular displays painstaking workmanship. The lid, which was probably made of pine because poplar was not obtainable in that width, has end cleats in breadboard style. It folds on square hinges between the slanted portions of the desk ends.

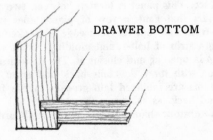

DRAWER BOTTOM

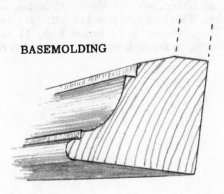

BASEMOLDING

102

All exposed board edges are finished with a 5/16 inch single-arch molding set flush with the inner face. The slides that support the fall front are almost square in section, and are equipped with small, cast-brass knobs. The space between the upper drawers and the desk bottom into which these slides disappear is accessible through a sliding panel in the desk writing surface. This panel is located between two pairs of drawers that flank a row of pigeonholes under the fall-front and top. Its front edge is marked by a full-length strip of half-round molding which serves as a grip in opening and closing it. The desk drawers are made with three dovetails back and front, and the bottoms are rabbeted into grooves in the front, sides, and back, as shown in the sketch.

The tombstone-shaped panels of the cupboard are of a very early type with wide chamfers. The pinning was obviously very carefully done, the pins being staggered to reduce the possibility of splitting the stiles. Only the meeting stile of the right-hand door is beaded, and this also has a quarter-round lip that overlaps a narrow rabbet on the other door. These doors are hung on handmade wrought-iron hinges. Another important feature of the top is the cornice which not only rises ¾ inch above the cupboard top, but is elaborately molded and heavy enough to nicely balance the base. Note that all four feet are ball turnings.

Over-all dimensions are: Height 72 inches, width 36 inches. The desk is 42 inches tall, 18½ inches deep. The cupboard is 30 inches high, 11 inches deep, resting on the desk top which 9¼ inches deep.

103

FOLDING DESK

This portable item is only 27¾ inches high and presumably is a field desk, though it has no carrying handles or any cover for the lower part. The use of early-style butterfly hinges suggests that it was made sometime in the early 18th century, but its chief claim to fame is the hinged top which folds down against the front, covering the upper compartments. There is, however, no apparent means of fastening the top in the dropped position.

The box is of panel construction, with posts of maple and the rest of pine. Let into each front post is an iron rod, ¼ inch square in section. Each rod can be tilted forward and its upper end inserted into a socket hole cut into the underside of the lid. At their lower end, the rods are kept from falling out by a metal lip forming the base of the slot. The ends of the desk are ½-inch boards let into the stiles and pegged almost flush with them. The slightly overlapping top carries a separately made rack that measures 8½ inches from front to back. In order that the hinged desk top can fold down flat against the stiles, its rear edge and the front edge of the top are both

cut away at an angle of 45 degrees. The top is a single board 24 inches long, 14 inches wide, with a strip of quarter-round molding at its lower edge to keep papers from sliding off. When closed, this board's bottom edge is in line with that of the box shelf. The two drawers in the bottom section are very simply made, with no more than a ⅛-inch lip. The back and sides are nailed on, and the bottom is nailed flush with them. Over-all dimensions are: 25⅜ inches long over the bottom molding, 27¾ inches tall, with 8½-inch sides.

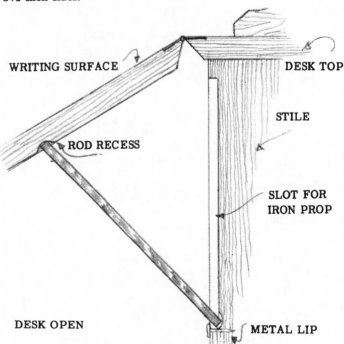

WRITING SURFACE

DESK TOP

STILE

ROD RECESS

SLOT FOR
IRON PROP

DESK OPEN

METAL LIP

INDEX

137